THE APPARENT DELAY

Arnold Valentin Wallenkampf

THE APPARENT DELAY

What Role Do We Play in the Timing of Jesus' Return?

REVIEW AND HERALD® PUBLISHING ASSOCIATION
HAGERSTOWN, MD 21740

This book was
Edited by Gerald Wheeler
Designed by Mark O'Connor
Typeset: Goudy 11/13

PRINTED IN U.S.A.

99 98 97 96 95 94   10 9 8 7 6 5 4 3 2 1

R&H Cataloging Service
Wallenkampf, Arnold Valentin, 1913-
     The apparent delay.

     1. Second Advent.   I. Title
          236.9

ISBN 0-8280-0735-7

Dedicated

Table of Contents

Preface and Acknowledgments

The second advent of Christ is a pivotal teaching of the New Testament. To the New Testament Christians it was "the blessed hope."

The strikingly conspicuous reemergence of this salient Christian hope during the first half of the nineteenth century gave rise to an Advent awakening. The New England States and surrounding areas witnessed the North American facet of this religious awakening. This New England Advent aAwakening spawned the Adventism from which the Seventh-day Adventist Church gradually developed.

The soon return of a visible, personal, and literal Saviour, just as the disciples saw Him ascend from the Mount of Olives, is one of the cardinal beliefs of the Seventh-day Adventist Church. This tenet, together with the observance of the seventh-day Sabbath, became part of its name—Seventh-day Adventist.

In certain circles of Seventh-day Adventism during the past few decades, a swirl of discussion has surged around the time of Christ's return. Seventh-day Adventists have always believed in Christ's soon return in glory. But today some staunchly assert that Christ's return should already have occurred. They maintain that it has been delayed partly by the church's neglect to more effectively proclaim Christ's gospel commission (Matt. 28:18-20), and partly by the church's present spiritual condition. Both factors have supposedly made it impossible for Jesus to return as planned. They think Jesus today is holding His return in abeyance, anxiously waiting for His people to get ready by individually more fully modeling their characters according to His will and by fulfilling the gospel commission.

Theologians and others interested in theology may be surprised by the number of anecdotes used here in this basically theological presentation. The writer, as he delved into the subject, weighed whether he should employ them, then remembered Jesus, the master teacher, preacher, and evangelist without a peer. About Him the evangelist Matthew wrote that "without a parable He did not speak to them" (Matt. 13:34).

The apostle Paul is the recognized theologian among the New Testament writers. But Jesus presented equally complicated subjects—for instance, justification by faith—just as lucidly or even more so in His parables. The story of the prodigal son offers a prime example. Abstract teaching is more difficult for both hearers and readers to grasp than parable teaching. To make the theme of this book more readily understood, I have felt that numerous anecdotes or illustrations were most appropriate.

I owe a great debt of gratitude to several friends who read the manuscript during its birth. Their suggestions were invaluable.

My greatest and most heartfelt thanks go to my wife, Mae. Without her help this book might never have come into existence. Its midwife, she brought it to the place where it saw the light of day by taking my—to some, indecipherable—hieroglyphics and putting them into beautiful English typescript. For this I owe her untold gratitude.

But special thanks go to the Review and Herald staff and its acquisitions editor Penny Wheeler who initiated the piloting of this manuscript through the shoals and narrows toward publication. Richard Coffen furnished encouragement and help. The final editor, Gerald Wheeler, did a magnificent job together with able copy editors in readying it for the press.

CHAPTER 1

The Apostles' Advent Hope

During the Desert Storm operation in the Persian Gulf, Sue's thoughts were almost constantly on Jack. For educational reasons he had enlisted in the Army several years earlier. He had reached his educational goal, and when Desert Shield began, he had a good job and enjoyed life with his little family, consisting of his wife, Sue, and 5-year-old Andrew and 3-year-old Kay.

But then the military summoned Jack to form part of Desert Shield, leaving Sue and the two small children alone. Desert Storm soon followed. The anxiety Sue experienced during Desert Shield had been bad enough, but nothing compared with what she went through when the bombing and shooting began. Now she was worried about Jack's life. She eagerly hoped that Desert Storm would soon be over and Jack would come back unscathed. After all, he was her husband—her best friend and her lover—the father of their two children. So she yearningly hoped and longed for his soon and safe return.

Sue's thoughts and feelings mirrored those of the eleven disciples for Jesus after He had ascended. Their best Friend had just left them. But they were not discouraged. Forty days earlier they had been devastated. All their hopes had faded with the Master's anguished cry "My God, My God, why have You forsaken Me?" (Mark 15:34). With His expiring breath their dreams had vanished and died.

But not so now. As they returned to Jerusalem after seeing their Master ascending into heaven, people stared at them in amazement. Their faces did not mirror defeat, but were animated with gladness and triumph. Heavenly happiness glowed from their features as they uttered praises and thanksgiving to God. They expressed no fear of the future. "They knew that Jesus was in heaven, and that His sympathies were with them still. They knew that they had a friend at the throne of God."[1]

The hearts of the eleven disciples returning from the Mount of Ascension were filled with courage and vibrant hope. His promise resounded in their minds: "In My Father's house are many mansions; if it were not so, I would have told you. I go to prepare a place for you. And if I go and prepare a place for you, I will come again and receive you to Myself; that where I am, there you may be also" (John 14:2, 3). Jesus had spoken those words to them Thursday evening shortly before His Gethsemane experience.

At their Passover celebration earlier that evening, He had introduced them to the Communion service. The apostle Paul later wrote about it: "For as often as you eat this bread and drink this cup, you proclaim the Lord's death till He comes" (1 Cor. 11:26). The ceremony was designed to keep the hope of His second coming ever after vivid in their minds. The eleven disciples were the first to cherish the Christian Advent hope.

Each time the early followers of Jesus drank the Communion wine, it directed their gaze forward to Christ's return. They remembered the words of Jesus: "Drink from it, all of you. For this is My blood of the new covenant, which is shed for many for the remission of sins. But I say to you, I will not drink of this fruit of the vine from now on until that day when I drink it new with you in My Father's kingdom" (Matt. 26:27-29).

The Communion service became a time of rejoicing. In the preparatory service of foot washing, the participants thought of their past shortcomings, confessed their wrongdoings, and let Jesus take them all away. As they ate the bread and drank the wine, they no longer stood in the shadow of the cross, but in its saving and life-giving light. They stood before their God with mind cleansed from all sin and personal grudges and resentments—arrayed in the garment of Christ's righteousness, perfect through their beloved Saviour. As they drank the juice from the vine, they remembered their Friend Jesus. And they looked forward to His coming to take them to His Father's home, beyond sorrow, suffering, temptation, sin, and even death. And then He Himself would again share the Communion wine with them.

With the Advent hope glowing in their hearts, and stimulated every time they ate the Communion bread and drank its wine, the apostles often spoke of the nearness of the Second Advent. They expressed their belief in Christ's return to earth in accordance with His promise. The most common word they used was *parousia*, which really means "coming" or "presence." The apostle Paul employed it several times in referring to human events. For example, he spoke about the *parousia* of Titus (2 Cor. 7:6) and of Stephanas (1 Cor. 16:17). He used it about his own visit to the believers of Philippi (Phil. 1:26; 2:12). And he even chose the word to describe his own allegedly weak "bodily presence" among the Corinthians (2 Cor. 10:10).

Secular Greek employed *parousia* for the widely heralded and trumpeted arrival of a king or emperor. In the New Testament it often denotes Christ's second advent.

The apostles believed that they were living in the last days and that Jesus would return in the lifetime of at least some of them, a belief reflected in their writings. They considered time to be extremely short, reminiscent of Adam and Eve, who hoped their first son would be the promised Saviour from sin.

A phrase a few New Testament writers used in referring to Christ's second advent is the "day of the Lord" (Acts 2:20). Peter first employed it in his sermon during the feast of Pentecost. To him the first coming of Jesus had occurred "in these last times" (1 Peter 1:20). In his Pentecostal sermon the disciple quoted Joel's prophecy of last-day events. The outpouring of the Holy Spirit he had witnessed among Jesus' followers represented to him a sign that he was actually living in the last days (see Acts 2:17-21). After healing the man lame from birth, he probably had the return of Jesus in mind when he mentioned the "restoration of all things" (Acts 3:21) to those who flocked around John and him at the Temple.

Peter's Epistles further reflect his belief in the nearness of Christ's second advent. He wrote that "the end of all things is at hand" (1 Peter 4:7) and that "the time has come for judgment to begin with the household of God" (verse 17, RSV). The disciple expected "the Chief Shepherd," Jesus, soon to appear. Then, he assured the faithful, "you will receive the crown of glory that does not fade away" (1 Peter 5:4).

In his Second Epistle, Peter commented on how unbelievers were mocking Christians whose hope of Christ's coming had not yet materialized (see 2 Peter 3:1-7). It shows that the Christians, just 30 years after the death and ascension of Jesus, had already expected His return in glory. The unbelievers implied that inasmuch as Jesus had not yet appeared, He would never come.

The apostle James also believed in the soon return of Jesus. To that end he admonished his fellow believers to be patient and wait like a farmer for his crop, "for the coming of the Lord is at hand" (James 5:8; see verse 7).

The apostle Paul likewise revealed his conviction of the soon return of Jesus in a number of his epistles. In the first of his epistles—1 Thessalonians, written around A.D. 51—he expressed his belief that at least some of the recipients of his letter would still be alive at the Second Advent when he wrote that "we who are alive and remain [until the coming of the Lord] shall be caught up" (1 Thess. 4:17; see verse 15). Each of the five chapters of 1 Thessalonians concludes with a reference to the second advent of Christ, conveying the conviction that Jesus' return was very near.

Because of his references to Christ's second coming, some Thessalonian believers gained the erroneous impression that Jesus would show up immediately. To correct the misapprehension, Paul addressed another Epistle to them, cautioning them not to expect the Advent until the man of lawlessness would appear and other important developments would happen (see 2 Thess. 2:1-12). Paul knew that the gospel commission (see Matt. 24:14; Mark 13:10) must first be fulfilled. But when he wrote his Epistle to the Colossians, around A.D. 62, he held that Christians had already accomplished it (Col. 1:6, 23).

Paul firmly believed that Jesus' return was near. In keeping with his conviction, he counseled the unmarried Corinthian believers that it would be wiser not to marry, for "the time is short, so that from now on even those who have wives should be as though they had none" (1 Cor. 7:29; see verses 25-27). In fact, because of the nearness of Christ's coming, it would be better for even the married to live celibate lives. The believers' attention should focus on the second advent of Jesus (see 1 Cor. 1:7). To Paul the nearness of the Lord's coming was so close that all believers should keep it constantly in mind. Paul verily believed that he was living at "the ends of the ages" (1 Cor. 10:11).

Other Epistles of his also witness to his conviction in the nearness of the Second Advent. "The night is far spent, the day is at hand," he wrote in Romans 13:12. Philippians stresses that the day of "the Lord is at hand" (Phil. 4:5; cf. 1:6, 10; 2:16). The apostle's treasured hope was the soon appearance of Jesus, a position that he constantly shared with his fellow believers.

"Paul was an Adventist; he presented the important event of the second coming of Christ with such power and reasoning that a deep impression, which never wore away, was made upon the minds of the Thessalonians."[2]

The Epistle to the Hebrews affirms that the day of the Lord's return was near at the time of its composition. "For yet a little while, and He who is coming will come and will not tarry" (Heb. 10:37; cf. verse 38 and Heb. 9:28). The writer consequently calls his times or the time Jesus spent on earth "these last days" (Heb. 1:2).

The beloved apostle John, who outlived all the other apostles, believed to his dying day in the Lord's soon return. He was convinced that he was living in "the last hour" (1 John 2:18) of earth's history. The presence of the spirit of antichrist in the church (cf. 1 John 2:18 with 1 John 4:3) foretold by his fellow apostle Paul [see 2 Thess. 2:7-9] as a sign of the nearness of the end) John saw as further evidence for his conviction.

In His revelation to John on the penal island of Patmos, Jesus testified to the nearness of His coming when He declared through John, "The time is at hand" (Rev. 1:3, KJV). In Revelation 3:11 Jesus Himself assures the church in Philadelphia of His soon return: "Behold, I come quickly! Hold fast what you have, that no one may take your crown." In the very last chapter of Revelation, Jesus reiterates three times: "I am coming quickly!" (Rev. 22:7, 12, 20).

The threefold assurance of His soon advent was sweet music in the ears of John, who, with the other apostles, had ardently longed for His return ever since he saw Him ascend to heaven. John's answer to Jesus' promise was "Amen. Even so, come, Lord Jesus!" (verse 20).

It was God's plan that the "promise of Christ's second coming was ever to be kept fresh in the minds of His disciples."[3] And the disciples were true stewards of the mysteries of God. They never forgot their Master's promise to take them to the mansions He had gone to prepare for them in His Father's house. Each one lived and worked with the cherished hope of his best Friend's soon return, maintaining "an attitude of constant expectancy."[4]

The Advent hope in the hearts of the disciples was to be echoed throughout the ages by sincere Bible students.

---

[1] Ellen G. White, *The Desire of Ages*, p. 833.
[2] ———, *Sketches From the Life of Paul*, p. 83.
[3] ———, *The Acts of the Apostles*, p. 33.
[4] ———, *The Desire of Ages*, p. 632.

CHAPTER 2

Glimpses of the Advent Hope Throughout Christian History

During my years of teaching I knew college and graduate students who endured privations and hardships with undaunted courage. Even though at times some hardly had enough food, they did not despair. They kept their eyes on their goals and stuck by their courses of study with courage and hope, continuously buoyed up by the assurance that when they attained their educational goals, conditions would improve and life would be easier. The prospect gave them both mental and emotional steadfastness and the physical strength to cope without complaining amid adversity or even dire need.

The hope of Christ's second advent vitalized the experience of the disciples and their fellow believers, as it has throughout Christian history. It enabled them to be loyal to the Master despite trials, persecutions, and even martyrdom. Stephen, the first Christian martyr, faced death fearlessly with his eyes focused on Jesus as his soon-coming King (see Acts 7:55). All of the apostles except John followed him to a martyr's grave. And John too would have been a martyr if he had died when immersed in boiling oil prior to his exile to Patmos.

The apostles shared their ardent Advent hope with those around them. And others embraced it with the same eagerness with which the apostles themselves cherished it. To the New Testament Christians the glorious appearing of their great God and Saviour Jesus Christ became "the blessed hope" (Titus 2:13) daily energizing them.

With the Advent hope burning brightly in the hearts of the early Christians, they became, as Elton Trueblood called them, an "incendiary fellowship." Their hope lit the gospel fires throughout the whole Roman Empire. Under the symbol of a rider on a white horse, the New Testament believers "went out conquering and to conquer" (Rev. 6:2). Within a few centuries Christianity engulfed the empire, and even Roman emperors turned from paganism.

Men and women can endure almost anything when they have the hope and assurance of something better awaiting them in the future. That's the reason Karl Marx remarked that religion "is the opium of the people." His statement, though often derided by Christian believers, contains a vital truth. Opium was ranked as the most effective pain reliever until the development of morphine in the 1800s. Today we use many more powerful sedatives and pain-killers. An anesthetic relieves pain by removing the sensation of it.

As opium makes a person less sensitive to pain, so a commitment to Jesus with the belief that He is soon to come as king of the universe erases the fear of the most severe persecutions. A believer who knows that his or her Friend has "the keys of Hades and of Death" (Rev. 1:18) becomes invincible. The believer can face both torture and death with unconquerable fortitude, as the enduring faith of fellow believers under Communist or other oppressions has demonstrated again and again.

With the Second Advent hope, the believer realizes that physical death is not the end. Even in the moment of death he or she can, with Stephen, see Jesus, the Life-giver, at the right hand of God. To such men and women Jesus' words have indeed become reality: "And do not fear those who kill the body but cannot kill the soul. But rather fear Him who is able to destroy both soul and body in hell" (Matt. 10:28).

The apostle Paul pictured this sustaining source of strength when he wrote that "the sufferings of this present time are not worthy to be compared with the glory which shall be revealed in us" (Rom. 8:18). Such hope has its anchor in Jesus and His second advent.

Just as Christians have never forgotten Christ's first coming as a baby, so has the hope of His second advent glimmered throughout the centuries. These two events, one in the past, the other still future, have safely guided the Christian community through jungles of heresy and problems of every kind. Through all ages God has had His heroes of faith who have upheld and proclaimed His truth and been unashamed and unafraid to acknowledge themselves as His followers. They never lost courage because they knew they had a Friend in heaven who one day soon, they believed, would return to earth as King of kings and Lord of lords.

Ignatius, thought to have been a contemporary and a fellow disciple of John the Beloved, believed his were the last times. Early in the second century he declared in his epistle to the Ephesians that "the last times are come upon us." [1]

During the first half of the second century Barnabas exulted, "The Lord is near, and His reward." [2]

The apologist Justin Martyr, about the middle of the second century, witnessed to the two advents of Christ as the two foci in redemption history. He based his belief on the prophets, of whom he wrote: "For the prophets have proclaimed two advents of His: the one, that which is already past, when He came as a dishonoured and suffering Man; but the second, when, according to prophecy, He shall come from heaven with glory, accompanied by His angelic host." [3]

Cyprian, around A.D. 250, said, "Whatever things were predicted are fulfilled; and . . . the end of the world is approaching." [4]

The writings of Augustine, the influential Church Father (died A.D. 430), helped create a wave of expectation for Christ's second advent. He identified the church-state coalition as a manifestation of God's kingdom on earth. [5] From his idea arose the belief that the return of Jesus would occur around A.D. 1000. At first the expectation faded away as many realized the impossibility of a corrupt church preparing the world for God. But despite this, excitement resurged as the year 1000 itself approached.

Several hundred years later the writings of Joachim of Floris triggered a widespread expectation of the end of the world in 1260, and again in 1300, even though he himself had set no date.[6]

Luther, foremost among the Reformers, observed that the prophets spoke and preached of both Christ's first and second advents. And in his *Table Talk* he voiced his longing for the Second Advent in these words: "I hope the last day will not be long delayed."[7] He wished that it might be in his own day when he said, "Ah, loving God, come [at] once; I wait continually for that day. . . . The name of the Lord be praised, who hath taught us to sigh and yearn after that day. . . . I hope, truly, that day is not far off."[8]

In the midst of the throes of the Reformation, Luther cried out, "I ardently hope that, amidst these internal dissensions on the earth, Jesus Christ will hasten the day of His coming."[9]

Calvin likewise envisioned the second advent of Christ as the church's true hope. So "we must," he said, "hunger after Christ till the dawning of that great day when our Lord will fully manifest the glory of His kingdom. The whole family of the faithful will keep in view that day."[10]

With our greater knowledge of the Bible prophecies, we may justly wonder how the New Testament writers, their contemporaries, and their successors throughout the centuries could possibly expect the second advent to occur so soon after Christ's ascension. Did they not have the Old Testament time prophecies of 1260, 1335, and 2300 days, or prophetic years? The longest, the 2300-day prophecy, would take them down to 1844. So why did these worthies of faith expect Him so soon or even in their own day?

Yes, they did have the Old Testament with its time prophecies given to the prophet Daniel, a "man greatly beloved" (Dan. 10:11). But God also told Daniel that the prophecies were "closed up and sealed till the time of the end" (Dan. 12:9). In His mercy He did not unveil their meaning to Daniel, nor to many succeeding generations of Christians. Christians for nearly two millennia failed to discern the lapse of time before Christ's second advent.

The Old Testament Jews in the same way were blind to the time that must pass before the coming of the Messiah. Like them,

Christians of every succeeding generation unabashedly continued to expect Christ's soon return. The meaning of Daniel's time prophecies was hidden from the readers of his book as the meaning was from Daniel himself. In this way the Advent hope has always existed among God's people. For example, Adam and Eve started looking for the Redeemer as soon as they received the promise in Genesis 3:15. Every Jewish mother hoped her son might be the promised Redeemer. In the same way Christians have always watched for Christ's second advent ever since He ascended. Despite the apparently tardy fulfillment of the promise of His advents, the pious in both Old and New Testament times have never relinquished their hope.

With the expiration of the last time prophecy in 1844, the Advent believers, even after the October disappointment, confidently anticipated Christ's speedy return. In two of their leading papers, the Millerites published a confession in an "Address to the Public" in which they admitted they were disappointed. But they also stated: "We are, therefore, now occupying a period of time in which we are to take heed to ourselves, lest at any time our hearts be overcharged with surfeiting and drunkenness, and cares of this life, and so that day come upon us unawares. Our position, therefore, is one of continual and confident expectation. . . . It will be our purpose, the 'little while' we may continue here, to present the doctrine of the Advent in all its purity."[11]

William Miller himself, the father of the American Advent movement, until his death remained firm in the belief that the end could not be far off, and that Jesus would soon come. In a letter dated November 10, 1844, he wrote to Joshua Himes and all Adventists: "*Brethren*, hold fast; let no man take your crown. I have fixed my mind upon another time, and here I mean to stand until God gives me more light. And that is *Today*, *Today*, and *Today*, until He comes, and I see Him for whom my soul yearns."[12]

Miller was indeed a genuine Adventist—a member of the people of the Second Advent—until his death. He looked yearningly for his Master's return. His attitude was just like that of the apostle John when he wrote, "Even so, come, Lord Jesus!" (Rev. 22:20).

With the discovery of the sanctuary truth, the Sabbatarian

Adventists learned that the 2300-day prophecy did not terminate with Christ's second advent. But they nevertheless continued to wait for His imminent return. And Seventh-day Adventists have done so ever since.

I remember my maternal grandfather, who would come and visit us once or twice a year. Grandpa was a tall, strong-looking man. He and my grandmother had been Baptists before they accepted the Seventh-day Adventist message in the late 1800s.

What always comes to the fore when I think of Grandpa was his constant talk about the soon coming of Jesus, a theme uppermost in his thinking and his favorite subject of conversation.

Grandpa eagerly anticipated Christ's second advent. My grandparents were Adventists just like Paul and the other apostles had been. My mother and father too were Adventists. They cherished the Advent hope until their dying moments.

During the first part of the twentieth century the well-known English preacher and writer Dr. G. Campbell Morgan phrased his Advent hope in these words: "To me the Second Coming is the perpetual light on the path which makes the present bearable. I never lay my head on my pillow without thinking that maybe before the morning breaks, the final morning may have dawned. I never begin my work without thinking that perhaps He may interrupt my work and begin His own. This is now His word to all believing souls till He comes." G. Campbell Morgan was an Adventist.

The Advent hope is still alive. It lights up the path for Seventh-day Adventists—and many others—around the world today. It rests on the prophecies pointing to the nearness of Jesus' return.

---

[1] "Epistle of Ignatius to the Ephesians," Chap. XI, in *The Ante-Nicene Fathers*, Vol. I, p. 54. A brief summary of statements indicating belief in the nearness of the Second Advent throughout the centuries appears in Herbert Douglass, *The End* (Mountain View, Calif.: Pacific Press Pub. Assn., 1979), pages 168-175.

[2] "The Epistle of Barnabas," Chap. XXI, *The Ante-Nicene Fathers*, Vol. I, p. 149.

[3] "The First Apology of Justin," Chap. LII, *The Ante-Nicene Fathers*, Vol. I, p. 180.

[4] Cyprian, "Treatise I," par. 16, in *The Ante-Nicene Fathers*, Vol. V, p. 426.

[5] See Augustine, *The City of God*, Book XX, chap. 7; cf. Philip Schaff, *History of the Christian Church* (Grand Rapids: William B. Eardmans, 1967), vol. 2, pp. 619, 620.

[6] See LeRoy E. Froom, *The Prophetic Faith of Our Fathers* (Washington, D.C.:

Review and Herald Pub. Assn., 1946-1954), Vol. I, p. 903.

[7] Cited in the *SDA Bible Students' Source Book,* (Washington, D.C.: Review and Herald, Pub. Assn., 1962), p. 918.

[8] From *The Familiar Discourses of Dr. Martin Luther,* cited in the *SDA Bible Students' Source Book,* p. 920.

[9] Cited by John McNicol in "The Hope of the Church," and cited in the *SDA Bible Students' Source Book,* p. 916.

[10] *Ibid.*

[11] Cited by Francis D. Nichol in *The Midnight Cry* (Washington, D.C.: Review and Herald Pub. Assn., 1944), p. 263.

[12] *Ibid.*, p. 267.

CHAPTER 3

Prophecies Indicating the Nearness of Christ's Second Advent

ow close are we to the coming of Jesus? Some people believe it is imminent.

In *The USA Today* of Friday, June 21, 1991, an announcement in almost one-inch block letters in reverse print almost filled an entire page:

> "IN AUTUMN 1992,
> JESUS IS COMING AGAIN"

The eight subtitles, also in block letters in reverse print, began with "Hope of Jesus' Second Coming" and ended with "The Way to Eternal Life."

However, this *USA Today* alert did not advertise Christ's historical personal return as the two angels who talked to the disciples portrayed it. The angels said, "This same Jesus, who was taken up from you into heaven, will so come in like manner as you saw Him go into heaven" (Acts 1:11). Rather, the alarm in *USA Today* promoted the theory that teaches that "many who have waited eagerly for Jesus and lived holy and faithful lives will instantly be changed into holy bodies and raised up to meet the Lord in the air. Such a wonderful event is called 'rapture.'"

But Bible prophecies do indicate that Christ's historical, personal second advent is also near. Some sweep over large portions of human history and consist primarily of two kinds of approach. One group gives outline sequences of events without making any specific reference to the years covered. Others are time prophecies, or divinely inspired timetables.

We will first look at some prophecies involving long sequences of events. Two of them appear in chapters 2 and 7 of the book of Daniel. They stretch from the prophet's day until the end of the world.

Daniel 2 presents Nebuchadnezzar's dream of the metal image. Interpreting it, Daniel told the king that "you are this head of gold. But after you shall arise another kingdom . . . ; then another, a third kingdom. . . . [And] the [fourth] kingdom shall be divided" (verses 38-41).

The purpose of the dream was to show Nebuchadnezzar events through history, beginning with Babylon. Daniel told the king that in "the latter days" (verse 28), the time of the divided kingdom, "the God of heaven will set up a kingdom which shall never be destroyed; and the kingdom shall not be left to other people; it shall break in pieces and consume all these kingdoms, and it shall stand forever" (verse 44). The prophet ended his interpretation by saying that "the great God has made known to the king what will come to pass" (verse 45).

Daniel 7 consists of a picture prophecy of beasts—a lion, a bear, a leopard, and a nondescript creature—also outlining Babylonian and post-Babylonian history. The prophet explained that the beasts symbolize kings or kingdoms (see verses 17, 23).

The fourth beast gradually divided into 10 horns (see verses 23, 24). Among the 10 horns a little one arose, replacing three of the original ones (verse 8). This little horn grew and became dominant. The prophecy declares of it: "He shall speak pompous words against the Most High, shall persecute the saints of the Most High.

. . . But the court shall be seated, and they shall take away his dominion, to consume and destroy it forever. Then the kingdom and dominion, and the greatness of the kingdoms under the whole heaven, shall be given to the people, the saints of the Most High" (verses 25-27).

Both Daniel 2 and 7 set forth basic outlines of history from Daniel's day until the second advent of Jesus. Both outlines end with the establishment of the everlasting kingdom of God following the Second Advent.

From the time of Augustine (A.D. 354-430) Bible scholars have interpreted the different metals in the figure of Daniel 2 and the four beasts of Daniel 7 as standing for Babylon, Persia, Greece, and Rome.[1]

In the thirteenth century Thomas Aquinas (1225-1274), the *Doctor Angelicus* of the Catholic Church, identified the dominant horn as the antichirist.[2] John Wycliffe (1320-1384), "The Morning Star of the Reformation," followed Aquinas in interpreting the little horn as the antichrist of prophecy and equated it with the Papacy.[3] The prophetic interpretation of these symbols, arrived at before and on the eve of the Reformation, became the standard interpretation both of the Reformation and post-Reformation periods.

History has seen most of both prophecies fulfilled. Only the establishment of the kingdom of God in Daniel 2 and the taking away the dominion from the little horn power and the giving of it to "the saints of the Most High" foretold in Daniel 7:27 yet remain. Both events are reserved for the time of Christ's second advent.

The book of Revelation, the great apocalypse of the New Testament, has several outline prophecies. We will look at two examples: the seven churches, in chapters 2 and 3, and the seals, mainly in chapter 6.

The seven churches of Revelation 2 and 3 are commonly considered to "represent the universal church of all times and places,"[4] or "the church of Christ in every country of the world, down to the very end of time."[5]

Six of the seven churches have already passed off history's stage: Ephesus, Smyrna, Pergamos, Thyatira, Sardis, and Philadelphia. Today we live in the time of the seventh church. No other church is to follow.

The Seventh-day Adventist Church is part of the Laodicean church. With Laodicea the plan of salvation will reach its climax, and Jesus will come. Every sin that might stain our lives Jesus is eager to wash away with His shed blood. Everyone who chooses may be perfect in Him.

Proceeding to Revelation 6, we read under the sixth seal: "Behold, there was a great earthquake; and the sun became black as sackcloth of hair, and the moon became like blood. And the stars of heaven fell to the earth, as a fig tree drops its late figs when it is shaken by a mighty wind" (verses 12, 13). Jesus Himself referred to the same phenomena in the heavens (Matt. 24:29; Mark 13:24, 25; Luke 21:25) as omens of the nearness of His coming.

The foretold darkening of the sun occurred over New England and adjacent Canada on May 19, 1780. "It continued about 14 hours. . . . The darkness was so great that people were unable to read common print, or tell the time of day by their watches, or to dine, or transact their ordinary business without the light of candles. . . . The fowls retired to their roosts. Objects could not be distinguished but at a very little distance, and everything bore the appearance and gloom of night. The cause of these phenomena is unknown. They certainly were not the result of eclipses."[6]

An eyewitness, who saw in the unusual darkness a sign from God, wrote: "That this darkness was not caused by an eclipse is manifest, . . . for the moon was more than 150 degrees from the sun all that day. . . .

"It was undoubtedly a vast collection of . . . particles that caused the late uncommon darkness. . . .

"The primary cause must be imputed to Him that walketh through the circuit of heaven—who stretcheth out the Heaven like a curtain—who walketh upon the wings of the wind."[7]

In April 1943, 163 years later, a commentator observed: "They speak of it as the Dark Day, they whose forbears lived through the soul-stirring experience in 1780, echoes of which have come down through so many New England generations. It was a day in which countless thousands turned fearful eyes toward a sunless sky. . . . What awful portent was this? . . . Darkness invaded the Northeast without warning on Friday, the nineteenth of May, . . . about 10:00

in the morning and spread swiftly."[8]

Reporting the great meteor shower of November 13, 1833, the *New York Journal of Commerce* stated the following day: "No philosopher or scholar has told or recorded an event, I suppose, like that of yesterday morning. A Prophet 1,800 years ago foretold it exactly, if we will be at the trouble of understanding stars falling to mean falling stars, . . . in the only sense in which it is possible to be literally true."[9]

Scientists too were inspired by the dazzling display. Denison Olmstead, professor of astronomy at Yale, commented: "The attention of astronomers was particularly directed to the extraordinary shower of meteors which occurred on the 13th of November, 1833. I had the good fortune to witness these grand celestial fireworks, . . . an exhibition of the phenomenon called shooting stars. . . . The extent of the shower of 1833 was such as to cover no inconsiderable part of the earth's surface. . . . The flashes of light, although less intense than lightning, were so bright as to awaken people in their beds."[10]

To Professor Fletcher G. Watson, astronomer and leading authority on meteors at Harvard Observatory, the intensity of the celestial display was even more impressive than its geographical extent. In 1956 he wrote:

"A magnificent display of shooting stars startled the inhabitants of the Americas on November 13, 1833. Beginning before midnight, the meteors were as thick as flakes. A single observer often saw 20 appear within a second. . . . Many superstitious people thought this marked the end of the world and, as bells tolled, they prepared for the future."[11]

Chronologically preceding these sky writings of Revelation 6, the revelator placed a gigantic earthquake. Twenty-five years before the Dark Day, history had recorded "the Lisbon earthquake," so called because its submarine epicenter was near the Portuguese city of Lisbon. "Probably the most famous of all earthquakes is that which destroyed Lisbon on November 1, 1755. . . . Alexander von Humboldt states that the total area shaken was four times that of Europe."[12]

G. A. Eiby, geophysicist at the Seismological Observatory of Wellington, New Zealand, stated, "By far the most spectacular earthquake of earlier times was that of Lisbon, 1755. This has some claim to be regarded as the greatest earthquake on record."[13]

The series of natural phenomena thus started with the Lisbon earthquake in 1755, followed by the darkening of the sun on May 19, 1780 and the moon appearing like blood the following night. The falling of the stars occurred on November 13, 1833. The latter events, providentially visible in the northeastern United States, were especially regarded as a fulfillment of Revelation 6:12 and 13.

Verse 14 unveils the next event: "Then the sky receded as a scroll when it is rolled up, and every mountain and island was moved out of its place." This augurs the Second Advent, as Jesus Himself testified in Matthew 24:29, 30 and Mark 13:24-26.

In addition to these outline prophecies of happenings and events, God has placed time prophecies in His Word. They cover long periods, such as the 1260, 1290, 1335, and 2300 days of Revelation 12:6 (cf. 11:3); Daniel 12:11, 12; and Daniel 8:14, respectively (days here stand for years). Scripture several times refers to the 1260-day prophecy as "a time and times and half a time" (Dan. 7:25; 12:7; Rev. 12:14).

The first three time prophecies fall entirely within the Christian Era. Only the 2300-day prophecy covers a time span that began during the Jewish restoration period. This prophecy stretches more than 1,800 years into the Christian Era.

At the time of their writing and for a long time afterward, these prophecies did not mean much to God's people. They certainly were not understood. The angel Gabriel told Daniel to "shut up the words, and seal the book until the time of the end" (Dan. 12:4).

As a matter of fact, God does not hand us prophecies so that we can become expert prognosticators, or predictors, of future events. Rather, their purpose is to enable us to recognize foretold events when they occur (see John 13:19). Students of the Bible should permit time to be the interpreter. In keeping with this principle, it was only shortly before their fulfillment that devout people actually learned what these prophecies meant.

In this connection we will discuss only the 2300-day prophecy. The other three time prophecies all find their fulfillment within the time span of the 2300-day one.

The 2300-day prophecy covers a longer time span and comes closer to the Second Advent than any of the other three. In modern times Sir Isaac Newton (1642-1727) was the first prophetic interpreter to apply the year-day principle to the 70 weeks of Daniel 9. And the 70 weeks are the first part of the 2300-day prophecy. He placed their beginning in 457 B.C., based on Daniel 9.[14]

During the nineteenth century an avalanche of prophetic interpreters accepted and used the year-day principle.[15] In America William Miller and his colaborers accepted this now well-established pattern of prophetic interpretation. On this basis they expected Christ to come at the end of the 2300-day prophecy, the biblical time prophecy reaching furthest into modern times. Their interpretation eventually led them to expect Christ's return on October 22, 1844.

The failure to understand such time prophecies for centuries explains how the most faithful followers of Christ have always—throughout all ages—been able to cherish a most fervent Advent hope. But God's people could accurately grasp them only shortly before their actual completion.

All the great outline prophecies with their long sequences of epochs and events spanning the centuries have now run out. The prophetic time periods in the books of Daniel and Revelation have all expired, or been fulfilled. Jointly they announce the removal of these barriers to Christ's second advent.

> "The golden morning is fast approaching;
> Jesus soon will come
> To take His faithful and happy children
> To their promised home."

After Jesus left the Temple for the last time, He answered His disciples' query about its destruction. In His discourse He intermingled the destruction of the Temple and the fall of Jerusalem with the end of the world (see Matt. 24; Mark 13; Luke 21:5-36). "Take heed that no one deceives you," He warned the disciples. "For many will come in My name, saying, 'I am Christ.' . . . And you will hear of wars and rumors of wars. See that you are not troubled. . . . For nation will rise against nation, and kingdom against kingdom. And there will be famines, pestilences, and earthquakes in various places. . . . Then they will deliver you up to tribulation and kill you, and you will be hated by all nations for My name's sake. . . . And because lawlessness will abound the love of many will grow cold. . . . And this gospel of the kingdom will be preached in all the world as a witness to all the nations, and then the end will come' " (Matt. 24:4-14).

Christians from the earliest days have observed such events and read into them the nearness of Christ's second advent. These events nourished the hope of Christians in all ages that His coming was at hand. Jesus wanted all His followers, no matter when they lived, to have the continuous hope of His soon return. And for all of us individually, that has always been solemnly true. No one at any time throughout history has ever been any further than a heartbeat from the Second Advent.

As there is only one unfailing test of a true prophet—undeviating loyalty to God's Word (see Isa. 8:20)—so there is also but one absolute indication of the nearness of the end of time and Christ's second advent. According to Christ's own word, it is the preaching of the gospel in all the world (Matt. 24:14).

Without a doubt we are today close to that achievement. Radio and TV are circling the globe. Everyone will soon be within electronic earshot and be able to hear and view the proclamation of the gospel.

A family's sundial had inscribed on it the words "It Is Later Than You Think." The Christian's primary sundial is the Word of God—the Bible. It tells us that the second advent of Christ is near. One reliable witness wrote, "It will not tarry past the time that the message is borne to all nations, tongues, and peoples." [16]

Since 1844 people have been in an entirely different situation than pre-1844 generations. All the time prophecies have expired, removing all prophetic time restraints to Christ's second advent. Jesus is soon to come.

Some ascribe special significance to Luke 21:24. Part of it reads: "Jerusalem will be trampled by Gentiles until the times of the Gentiles are fulfilled." While it is not a time prophecy, it does pinpoint a happening comparable to the gospel going to all the world

(Matt. 24:14). At the Bible conference held in Takoma Park, Maryland, in September 1952, Elder Arthur S. Maxwell, longtime editor of the *Signs of the Times*, called special attention to this prophecy. He alerted all Seventh-day Adventists to watch it with special care.

"For nineteen centuries Jerusalem has been trodden down of the Gentiles," he declared. "It is still trodden down of the Gentiles. Despite the amazing prowess of the Israeli troops, the ancient city of Jerusalem is still in Arab hands. A Mohammedan mosque still stands upon the site of Solomon's Temple. Victorious as were the forces of Israel in every other part of Palestine, they failed to take the most dazzling objective of all. Mysteriously they were held back from achieving this most cherished goal, this culminating triumph, as by an unseen hand.

"What could be the reason? Only that the times of the Gentiles are not yet fulfilled."[17]

During the Six-Day War in June 1967, Israeli troops gained that "most dazzling objective of all." Jerusalem fell into the hands of the Israelis after more than 1,900 years under Gentile rule. "Jerusalem here [in Luke 21:24] constitutes the last sign of the times by which the Lord shows us that the history of this world is coming to its climax and that the restoration of all things is at hand," Jean R. Zurcher observed.[18]

With the rise of the Christian church the Jews—or ancient Israel—were no longer God's chosen people, or nation. Nevertheless Jesus told His disciples that when Roman armies surrounded Jerusalem, it would be a sign for God's people to leave the city (see Matt. 24:15, 16). So in the end-time the fate of Jerusalem—the end of Gentile control of it—would again be a sign for God's people to be ready for the end of probationary time, an alert that Jesus is soon to come.

In the words of F. E. Belden:

"We know not the hour of the Master's appearing;
  Yet signs all foretell that the moment is nearing
  When He shall return—'tis a promise most cheering—
  But we know not the hour."

[1] See L. E. Froom, *The Prophetic Faith of Our Fathers*, Vol. I, p. 894.

[2] *Ibid.*, p. 656.

[3] *Ibid.*, Vol. II, pp. 52-54, 156, 157.

[4] R. R. Jamieson, A. R. Fausset, and D. Brown, *Commentary*, "Revelation," chapter 1, verse 4, and chapter 2, verses 1-29.

[5] William Milligan, *The Book of Revelation*, in *The Expositor's Bible*, pp. 5, 6.

[6] Robert Sears, ed., *The Guide to Knowledge*, p. 428.

[7] Samuel Stearns, letter in *Independent Chronicle* (Boston), June 22, 1780.

[8] John Nicholas Beffel, "Dark Day in England," *American Mercury*, April 1943, pp. 481-485.

[9] Nov. 14, 1833, p. 2.

[10] Cited in *The American Journal of Science and Arts* 25 (1834): 363-365.

[11] *Between Planets*, rev. ed. (Cambridge, Mass.: Cambridge University Press, 1956), p. 95.

[12] Perry Byerly, "Earthquakes," *Encyclopedia Britannica* (1961 ed.), vol. 7, p. 848.

[13] *About Earthquakes* (New York: Harper, 1957), pp. 141, 142.

[14] See Froom, Vol. II, pp. 662, 664.

[15] See Froom, Vol. III, pp. 744, 745.

[16] Ellen G. White, *Evangelism*, p. 697.

[17] *Our Firm Foundation* (Washington, D.C.: Review and Herald Pub. Assn., 1953), Vol. II, p. 230.

[18] J. R. Zurcher, *Christ of the Revelation* (Nashville: Southern Pub. Assn., 1980), pp. 71, 72.

CHAPTER 4

Ellen White Believed in the Nearness of Christ's Second Advent

On October 22, 1844, in Portland, Maine, 16-year-old Ellen Harmon (White, after August 1846) confidently waited with other followers of William Miller for Jesus to come. Similar groups had gathered throughout New England and neighboring states in churches or in private homes to greet Jesus' return. At the Miller farm in Low Hampton, New York, believers had assembled on the protruding rocks a short distance from the family home to catch a first glimpse of their arriving Saviour.[1]

Ellen had first heard "The Advent Near" in March 1840 and then again in June 1842. On both occasions William Miller preached at the Casco Street Christian Church in Portland. She listened to him with keen interest and accepted his message with members of her family and friends. For doing so the Harmon family with others found themselves disfellowshipped from the Chestnut Street Methodist Church in 1843. But her love for Jesus grew and deepened. Thinking back on her 1844 experience, she later wrote: "This was the happiest year of my life. My heart was full of glad expectation. . . . My faith was unclouded, and I appropriated to myself the precious promises of Jesus."[2] She looked forward to October 22 with joy.

But after it had come and gone, "it was a bitter disappointment that fell upon the little flock whose faith had been so strong and whose hope had been so high. But we were surprised that we felt so free in the Lord, and were so strongly sustained by His strength and grace. . . . We were disappointed, but not disheartened."[3] She and the other Advent believers were deeply in love with the Lord, and fervent love and discouragement are mutually exclusive.

Ellen's hope of seeing Jesus ride forth on the clouds of glory in October 1844 failed. But that did not quash her faith in the soon return of Jesus. Throughout her long life she nurtured ardent love for Jesus. And her love went hand in hand with her belief in His soon coming. She—with many other Adventists—believed she would soon see Him arrive in glory as King of kings and Lord of lords to gather His own to Himself in His eternal kingdom of love and peace.

Ellen White belonged to the small group of Advent believers who neither despaired because of their unfulfilled hopes nor turned to fanaticism. They clung to their faith in God and His leading and became Seventh-day Adventists. She, with the others, kept her eyes steadfastly focused on Jesus. They could do so because they had gone through an experience with Him. At peace with their Saviour, they possessed assurance of salvation by grace through faith.

Each of them was animated by the hope that the prophet Isaiah put into words: "Behold, this is our God; . . . we have waited for Him; we will be glad and rejoice in His salvation" (Isa. 25:9).

Her hope of Christ's soon return never wavered nor faded. In *Experience and Views,* first published in 1851, she wrote: "Some are looking too far off for the coming of the Lord. Time has continued a few years longer than they expected. . . . I saw that the time for Jesus to be in the most holy place was nearly finished and that time can last but a very little longer."[4] It remained the tenor of her messages to the Advent believers for the next 64 years.

Throughout her long life Ellen White lived with the firm conviction that Jesus was soon to come. He and His soon advent anchored her Christian belief to her dying day.

Ellen White's belief in the nearness of Christ's appearance rested on her understanding of the Scriptures. With other Seventh-day Adventists, she recognized that all the time prophecies had expired. She knew that she and her fellow believers, as are we, were living in the end-time. Her message regarding the nearness of the end of time never changed. It rang the same throughout her entire life. Statements from later decades of her life will demonstrate her unwavering conviction:

In *Testimony* 1, first published in 1855, Ellen White told her fellow believers, "I saw that we should not put off the coming of the Lord."[5]

Thirteen years later (1868) she stated that "the coming of the morning to the faithful, and of the night to the unfaithful, is right upon us."[6]

Testimony 28, first published in 1879, declared, "We are now upon the very borders of the eternal world."[7]

As she closed her sermon on the first Sabbath of the 1888 General Conference, she said, "Now, brethren, we are almost home."[8]

While in Australia (1891-1900) Ellen White wrote, "The end is near! . . . Jesus will soon come. Let men see that we believe that we are on the borders of the eternal world."[9]

Ellen White's fervor in proclaiming the nearness of the Lord's return did not abate as she approached the end of her life. She expressed her settled conviction in 1904 that "the end is very near."[10] Her Week of Prayer reading for Sabbath, December 9, 1905, began with her familiar words "The Lord is soon to come."[11]

In 1908, seven years before her death in 1915, her message had not changed. "Let every human intelligence who professes the name of Christ testify: 'The end of all things is at hand; prepare to meet thy God.'"[12]

We could cite numerous similar statements from Ellen White's pen as she believed that the events of her time were omens of the nearness of the end and the approach of Jesus. She was like the apostles and Christians throughout all ages who also read the nearness of the end in the events transpiring around them. The apostle John, for example, was convinced that he was living in the last hour, because many antichrists had come (1 John 2:18; cf. Heb. 1:2).

In 1903 Ellen White appealed to "many in our churches" "not to disregard the fulfilling of the signs of the times, which say so plainly that the end is near."[13] Firmly she believed they were living amid the closing scenes of human history.

To Ellen White the early 1900s seemed to augur the end. "Troublous times are right upon us. The signs of the times reveal that the day of the Lord is soon to come. . . . Strikes are common. Thefts and murders are committed on every hand. Men possessed by demons are killing men and women and little children. The taking of human life is a matter of daily occurrence. All these things testify that the end of all things is at hand"[14]

When some critics chided her for continuously proclaiming the nearness of Christ's return for many years, she replied: "The angels of God in their messages to men represent time as very short. Thus it has always been presented to me. It is true that time has continued longer than we expected in the early days of this message. Our Saviour did not appear as soon as we hoped. But has the Word of the Lord failed? Never!"[15]

Another phrase Ellen White often used to convey the imminence of Christ's second advent in her times was "the last days." Prophetically speaking, she was correct. She, with her fellow believers in the Advent message, knew that prophetic time had run out. The longest time prophecy—the 2300-day prophecy—had expired in 1844. As far as time prophecies indicated, Jesus might come at any moment. To that end, she spoke repeatedly about living in the last days. As a result she wrote that "the prophetic reckoning shows us that Christ is at the door."[16]

The New Testament writers, being blissfully unaware of the meaning of the time prophecies, could apply the same term to their own days. To them all time after the cross was the last days, as it is to many New Testament scholars today.

In *The Great Controversy*, Ellen White quoted the following verses: "'Cast not away therefore your confidence, which hath great recompence of reward. For ye have need of patience, that, after ye have done the will of God, ye might receive the promise.

For yet a little while, and he that shall come will come, and will not tarry. Now the just shall live by faith: but if any man draw back, my soul shall have no pleasure in him. But we are not of them who draw back unto perdition; but of them that believe to the saving of the soul' (Heb. 10:35-39, KJV)." Then she added, "That this admonition is addressed to the church in the last days is evident from the words pointing to the nearness of the Lord's coming: 'For yet a little while, and he that shall come will come, and will not tarry.' "[17]

A passage written to the New Testament believers, Ellen White applied with equal force to her generation.

All through her life she firmly believed that she, with her generation, was treading on the brink of eternity. But she never succumbed to the temptation to set a date for Christ's return. She adamantly opposed time-setting.

Jesus let His disciples know that the moment of His return "was not the thing of most importance for them to know."[18] Ellen White reminded her fellow believers that it was also true of them. "Instead of exhausting the powers of our mind in speculations in regard to the times and seasons which the Lord has placed in His own power, and withheld from men, we are to yield ourselves to the control of the Holy Spirit, to do present duties, to give the bread of life, unadulterated with human opinions, to souls who are perishing for the truth."[19]

To her the nearness of the end of all earthly things was an incentive for a personal commitment to Christ. It went back to her own experience of embracing the Advent message when preached by William Miller at the Christian Church on Casco Street during the early 1840s. She responded to the news of Jesus' soon return with ardent longing for His coming. Rather than fading away over the years, that longing grew and became stronger. And she hoped that everyone might respond in the same way. Thus throughout her long life she herself always believed—in harmony with Christ's Word—that His coming was near.

But how does God reckon time? Does He regard it as we do?

---

[1] According to the oral tradition in the Miller family.

2 Ellen G. White, *Life Sketches*, pp. 59, 60.

3 *Ibid.*, p. 61.

4 ———, *Early Writings*, p. 58.

5 ———, *Testimonies*, vol. 1, p. 123.

6 *Ibid.*, vol. 2, p. 194.

7 *Ibid.*, vol. 4, p. 306.

8 ———, cited in A. V. Olson, *Thirteen Crisis Years* (Washington, D.C.: Review and Herald, Pub. Assn., 1981), p. 277.

9 ———, *Testimonies*, vol. 6, pp. 436, 437.

10 *Ibid.*, vol. 8, p. 28.

11 ———, "The Time of the End," *Review and Herald*, Nov. 23, 1905.

12 ———, *Testimonies*, vol. 9, p. 62.

13 ———, "Sowing Beside All Waters," *Review and Herald*, July 14, 1903.

14 ———, in *(Australasian) Union Conference Record*, Jan. 15, 1904.

15 ———, *Selected Messages*, book 1, p. 67.

16 ———, *Manuscript Releases*, vol. 10, p. 270.

17 ———, *The Great Controversy*, pp. 407, 408.

18 ———, *Selected Messages*, book 1, pp. 185, 186.

19 *Ibid.*, p. 186.

CHAPTER 5

Time in God's Eyes and Ours

Long" and "short" are both relative depending upon what they qualify or refer to. If we apply the words to vacation trips, a long journey may denote thousands of miles; a short one, hundreds. If they refer to lumber, a long board may be anywhere from 8 to 16 or more feet, while a short one may be only a couple feet long. Or if we are speaking about tests, or examinations, a long examination may last anywhere from one to four or five hours, while a short test may involve only minutes.

In thinking of the time for Christ's second advent, we are dealing with time as God sees it. And with God even a thousand years is a short time, as we learn from the apostle Peter (see 2 Peter 3:8).

As humans we are by nature self-centered. Self-centeredness most clearly shows up in babies and small children. Their thoughts involve only themselves and their needs and desires. As a person grows and matures, we expect that he or she will outgrow egocentricity. The individual must curb or at least hide ego-centeredness in order to live effectively with other people.

A growing Christian matures so that he or she becomes God-centered rather than self-centered. God and His thoughts, God and His plans (His cause) and will, will become the center of the Christian's interest rather than self. The Christian fails God if he or she remains self-centered. The Church Father Tertullian observed about A.D. 200 that "he who lives only to benefit himself confers on the world a benefit when he dies." In the mature Christian the impulse to help others will constantly arise.

One expression of self-centeredness that often continues throughout life is the use of self as a frame of reference in thinking of other people. But we often do not stop at measuring other people by ourselves or by our standards. We also tend to squeeze God into conformity with our concepts.

And the concepts of God are almost as varied as human beings themselves. Most of us project our characteristics and even idiosyncrasies into Him. As a cabinetmaker builds any feature he likes into his own cabinet, so most of us tend to construct God according to the way we would like Him. We attribute to Him the qualities we like and think He ought to have. When it comes to time, most of us assume that God must measure it as we do, even though sin has dwarfed and cramped us.

But even if sin had never deformed humanity, men and women would never have become identical with God. They would have been perfect, made in the image of God, but not God—just as a baby is like its father or mother but a total replica of neither. We can never become carbon copies of God.

Nevertheless, as humans we are almost constantly trying to make God into our own image. For example, we circumscribe His nature by attributing to Him our human limitations. Almost unconsciously we also take for granted that God can see time only as we do.

But God is not like us. He is not made in our image, although originally He created us—mankind—in His. True, in some respects we are like Him. For instance, we can think and reason and make moral choices. In the process of human procreation, or reproduction, we create, or reproduce, other men and women as cocreators with God. But certainly we are not like God with reference to time.

God is bigger than time. Time exists in Him rather than He living in time as we do.

The Deity is the Creator and Maker of time, as of everything else. Time is a frame He established for Adam and Eve and their descendants to live in while they decided whether they would choose to be loyal to Him or not.

To us time exists in tenses—past, present, future. Not so with God. With Him there need be no difference between the past, the present, and the future. In one sense God is the everpresent now. Already, or now, He sees "us sit together in the heavenly places in Christ Jesus" (Eph. 2:6).

But God is not limited to a one-faced perennial "now" view of time. As humans we are prone to restrict Him to only one of the two options conceivable to us.

It is impossible for us to fathom God. We tend to encapsulate the Ever-existing One within an eternal present without allowing Him the possibility to observe daily happenings alongside His ability to envision future realities.

As a biblical Christian I sense no compulsion to imprison God within the bounds of my understanding, nor within the parameters of human logic and reason. My foundational Christian beliefs defy such a curtailment of God's potential. To believe that our Saviour, Emmanuel (God with us), was born of a virgin; to believe that Jesus was both true God and true man; to believe that He died and rose from the dead—such things do not make sense to rational human minds. Nor does the Christian belief in the Trinity conform to human logic. Fritz Guy appropriately speaks of "the inability of logic to function as the final judge of religious truth."[1] The same principle applies also to the truth about God.

I reject the notion that God's capacity and our religious beliefs must always conform to human logic and reason. To do otherwise is to suffer from the common human superstition that God is incapable of anything unacceptable to our human understanding. Unfortunately, if something God says violates our concept of reason and logic, we want to reject it. Unconsciously we insist on hemming God in with our human limitations.

Let us for a moment think of geometry. That study reinforced the concept in our minds that two parallel lines never meet. Having learned it as children, we saw it constantly verified by such things as the two rails of a railroad track. Therefore we readily accepted the theorem as axiomatic or absolutely true. However, as we continued to study we found that the parallel postulate is valid only in Euclidean, or plane, geometry—the only geometry most of us ever explored. But it does not apply in Riemannian geometry. The seemingly self-evident and inviolable theorem of parallelism is invalid in spherical geometry.

God has tried to explain to us His relationship to time—that in one sense He lives in the eternal present. When Moses asked the Lord what he should tell the Israelites when they asked who had sent him to deliver them from their Egyptian bondage, "God said to Moses, 'I am who I am.' This is what you are to say to the Israelites: 'I am has sent me to you'" (Ex. 3:14, NIV). He was trying to get across to Moses and his people that He is the Ever-existent One.

Through the Incarnation Jesus stepped out of eternity and entered time. Nevertheless He tried to impress His contemporaries with His eternal timelessness. When the Jews taunted Him that He was not yet 50 years old and still claimed to have seen Abraham, "Jesus said to them, 'Most assuredly, I say to you, before Abraham was, I AM'" (John 8:58).

Speaking both to Moses in Old Testament times and to His contemporaries in New Testament times, Jesus attempted to impress upon His hearers that God—the Father, the Son, and the Holy Spirit—sits enthroned above time.

In the A.D. 60s scoffers taunted Christians because their hopes of Christ's return had not yet materialized. Responding to the argument, Peter entered upon a discussion of God's concept of time. In 2 Peter 3:8 he emphatically said that the Lord does not view time as humans do. "Beloved," he said, "do not forget this one thing, that with the Lord one day is as a thousand years, and a thousand years as one day." Peter's point was that what may have seemed like a long time to the scoffers was not so with God.

God's thoughts are not ours (Isa. 55:8). Nor does God regard time as we do. The psalmist spoke of time in an interesting manner when he proclaimed, "For a thousand years in Your sight are like yesterday when it is past, and like a watch in the night" (Ps. 90:4).

Apart from His dealings with humanity, God apparently has no other time constraints. But in His concerns and dealings with our planet and the human race, time is vital and important, a fact we shall notice in the next chapter.

In the earth made new, time as we know it today will no longer exist. Its inhabitants will not count time in years, but nevertheless "'from one Sabbath to another, all flesh shall come to worship before Me,' says the Lord" (Isa. 66:23). While it sounds paradoxical, undoubtedly, with immortality and glorified bodies, we shall learn to interface moments with eternity.

With pleasant amusement I remember when our children were small. They had such confidence in their parents. They could not conceive of anything that Daddy or Mommy could not do. It was unimaginable to them that there was anything beyond our ability.

Small children have total confidence in their parents. When we ask our children to do something, we do not have to explain everything at their level of comprehension. They accept our words even though they do not understand. Their faith, trust, and confidence in us and what we say is full and complete. God hopes that our faith in Him and His Word might be equally that firm.

My mind cannot grasp many of the conundrums connected with God. Some of the enigmas contained in our current knowledge of God may never be solved until "He [God] will destroy on this mountain the surface of the covering cast over all people, and the veil that is spread over all nations" (Isa. 25:7). "For now we see in a mirror, dimly, but then face to face" (1 Cor. 13:12).

It takes humility on our part to accept what defies our understanding and eludes our logic and reasoning. Such humility little children possess. Jesus said about them, "Of such is the kingdom of heaven" (Matt. 19:14).

Lucifer, on the other hand, did not possess such humility. The Bible says that his "heart was lifted" (Eze. 28:17). Consequently, the being who had been perfect in his ways (verse 15) slowly transformed himself into the devil by exalting his reasoning and judgment above God's word.

At times I wonder why we are so insistent in bringing God

down to our level. We seem to be extremely uncomfortable with a Deity greater than we are. Perhaps J. B. Phillips' view that "your God is too small" applies even to many of us.

Western newcomers to the Orient may often regard Asians as inscrutable, unemotional, and beyond comprehension. But even though we might think that fellow inhabitants of our common globe are difficult to understand, we as Westerners assume that we can figure out God. We are not quite willing to concede that His ways are "past finding out" (Job 9:10; Rom. 11:33). But that is the testimony of both the Old and the New Testament.[2]

Children do not limit their parents' abilities to fit the confines of their present understanding. They take it for granted that their parents possess more resources and abilities than they can yet grasp. Implicitly trusting their parents, they readily concede that their parents are "past finding out."

I wonder at times how it would be if we as Christian believers would grant God that much room in our thinking. To give Him room to act as God rather than confine Him within the limits of human comprehension.

In the new earth the inhabitants will live in eternity. Sin-burdened measured time will then have fulfilled its purpose and will cease to exist. With the disappearance of time no one will ever grow old either chronologically or biologically, since the saved will then be partakers of immortality (see 1 Cor. 15:54).

People say that time passes quickly, especially when they reach an advanced age. But time really does not pass—it stands still. The passing of time is only an illusion.

We also say the sun rises and sets. But that also is an illusion. Rather it is the earth that constantly revolves. With reference to the earth, the sun stands still. And it is life that goes on and struggles. But time remains everlastingly still.

Humanity continuously advances from the cradle to the grave, year after year. Generation after generation lives and dies. But time in reality stands still, because time is part of eternity. Time frames the stages of the eons across which humanity wanders during its probationary period. Sound moves and perpetuates itself in waves. Fire does the same in iridescent flames. The air moves as a breeze.

But time stands everlastingly still, as frozen in ice, because time is a fraction of eternity.

God is fully aware of human concepts of time. He uses them in His dealings with humanity. "The centuries have their mission. Every moment has its work. Each is passing into eternity with its burden. . . . God is still dealing with earthly kingdoms. He is in the great cities. His eyes behold, His eyelids try, the doings of the children of men. We are not to say, God was, but, God is. He sees the very sparrow's fall, the leaf that falls from the tree, and the king who is dethroned."[3]

---

[1] Fritz Guy, in Clark H. Pinnock, ed., *The Grace of God, the Will of Man* (Grand Rapids: Zondervan Pub. House, 1989), p. 32.

[2] Some Bible translations, instead of using the phrase "past finding out" in Job 9:10, employ words like "unfathomable" (NASB), "incredible" (TLB), "beyond our ken" (Moffatt), "beyond understanding" (RSV), "cannot be fathomed" (NIV), or "cannot understand" (TEV).

[3] Ellen G. White, *Sons and Daughters of God*, p. 338.

CHAPTER 6

God's Timetable

All of us are acquainted with and have used timetables. The last one I looked at was one for an overseas flight from Baltimore-Washington International Airport to Stockholm, Sweden, by way of Amsterdam. It clearly gave the dates and departure and arrival times at the different airports.

In dealing with our world and its inhabitants, God has and uses timetables. But as humans we may not always be acquainted with them. So to us God seems often to be procrastinating when we think action is urgently needed. We often become impatient as we wait for Him to do something. The Bible presents several such occasions. Rebekah offers one example.

She was a good woman desirous that God's will would be done. Rebekah knew—as did Isaac—that God wanted Jacob to have the birthright. But her stubborn husband determined to give it to Esau. One day when Isaac told Esau to go and hunt for some game and prepare him a savory dish so that he might eat and bless his son, Rebekah decided she could wait no longer, and took things into her own hands. Jacob's mother reasoned that God desperately needed her help. "I am right here on the spot," she probably rationalized, "and God is far away. I'll do what I can to save the situation for Him."

To see God's will fulfilled in securing the birthright for her son, she resorted to deception. Craftily she persuaded Jacob to go in to his father and pretend to be Esau with the savory food that she had actually prepared.

When blind Isaac wondered whether Jacob were really Esau, as he claimed, the father had him approach so that he could feel him. With his hands and neck covered with the skins of the animals slaughtered for the savory food, Jacob felt like Esau. Only the voice was Jacob's, his father observed. And dressed in his brother's clothes, Jacob carried the fragrance of the wilderness, smelling like Esau. Mistaking Jacob for Esau, Isaac ate the food and blessed Jacob, thereby conferring the birthright on the younger son.

Inspiration comments that "God had declared that Jacob should receive the birthright, and His word would have been fulfilled in His own time had they [Rebekah and Jacob] waited in faith for Him to work for them. But like many who now profess to be children of God, they were unwilling to leave the matter in His hands."[1]

The prophet Habakkuk is another case in point. He demanded, "O Lord, how long shall I cry, and You will not hear? Even cry out to You, 'Violence!' And You will not save" (Hab. 1:2).

Habakkuk was upset that God did not punish wrongdoing in his native Judah. Because God remained silent, the prophet thought the Lord did not hear. But God both heard and had already planned for the cruel Babylonians to punish the kingdom of Judah for its sinfulness.

God had His own timetable for giving Jacob the birthright. But Rebekah was not willing to wait for Him to act. We have no idea when God would have given the younger son the birthright—but it would have happened. About 25 years passed between Habakkuk's urgent pleas for punishment on Judah for her sins and God's permitting Nebuchadnezzar to begin to punish her. Twenty more years elapsed before the final blow fell upon Jerusalem, ending in its destruction in 586 B.C. So apparently God has timetables for both daily happenings and historical events.

Even though God does not live in time, He is keenly aware of it, even in its small fractions, as is evident from His dealings with humans. He told Abraham that Sarah would bear him a son at a set time (Gen. 17:21). And a male child was to be circumcised on its eighth day (verse 12).

But God also recognizes longer time periods for historical events. He told Noah to build an ark to save those loyal to Him when He planned to send a flood upon the earth after 120 years (see Gen. 6:3, 14, 17). Within this period God knew that every person then living on earth would make an irreversible decision for or against Him.

In promising Abraham's descendants the land of Canaan, God mentioned a time constraint of 400 years (Gen. 15:13, 18). And God remembered His promise. After a lapse of 400 years the Lord freed His people from Egyptian bondage. "That very day the Lord brought the Israelites out of the land of Egypt, company by company" (Ex. 12:51, NRSV). (The apostle Paul in Galatians 3:17 speaks of it as a 430-year period. But his calculation rests on an earlier beginning date.)

The Jewish captivity in Babylon was to last 70 years (see Jer. 25:11). And it did, stretching from Nebuchadnezzar's first capture of Jerusalem in 605 B.C. (see Dan. 1:1, 2), to the proclamation of liberty by King Cyrus (see 2 Chron. 36:22, 23) in 536 B.C., inclusive reckoning.

God tied the birth of Jesus—the First Advent—firmly to a specific point in time. As soon as Adam and Eve in Eden received the promise of a Deliverer from sin, they began looking for Him. Joyfully they welcomed the birth of their first son, hoping he might be the fulfillment of the divine promise. Although the manifestation of the promise tarried, each succeeding generation cherished the hope of the Messiah. Enoch, in waiting for the Messiah, walked with God by faith (see Gen. 5:24; Heb. 11:5) for 300 years after the birth of his son Methuselah (Gen. 5:22).

But millennia passed by, and in the days of Ezekiel the Jews said forlornly, "The days are prolonged, and every vision fails" (Eze. 12:22). Doubting the reliability of both God's threats and promises, they felt bereft of hope, despairing of any prophetic fulfillment of the Messiah's coming. "But in heaven's council the hour for the coming of Christ had been determined,"[2] Ellen White reminds us. And Daniel, a contemporary of Ezekiel, announced the moment for the Messiah's arrival in history (see Dan. 9:24-27).

For Jesus to enter upon His ministry according to God's timetable announced by Daniel, "God sent forth His Son" "when the fullness of the time had come" (Gal. 4:4). At the beginning of His ministry Jesus said, "The time is fulfilled, and the kingdom of God is at hand" (Mark 1:15). "Messiah the Prince" came at the end of the 69 weeks and terminated His earthly ministry in the middle of the seventieth week, as Daniel had foretold.

It seemed to both pious antedeluvians and Jews for centuries that the Messiah's coming had been delayed. But that was not the case. It occurred at the exact moment in time according to heaven's timetable, even though the Jews, God's chosen people, had almost despaired of seeing the promise fulfilled. When He finally did arrive, after such a long delay according to their thinking, "the Jewish people were so engrossed with their own ambitious plans that they knew not of His advent."[3]

Both the beginning and the end of Christ's ministry on earth were anchored at specific points in history. But so was every day of His human life. The Holy Spirit guided Jesus step by step in His Father's will. For example, God had a specific moment for Him to perform His first miracle.

When His mother urged Him to do something when the wedding in Cana ran out of liquid refreshment, Jesus replied, "My hour has not yet come" (John 2:4). But shortly afterward it was time for Him to act, so He turned water into wine.

Another time when His brothers tried to encourage Him to go up to the Feast of Tabernacles at Jerusalem, "Jesus said to them, 'My time has not yet come. . . . You go up to this feast. I am not yet going up to this feast, for My time has not yet fully come'" (John 7:6-8). But shortly after His brothers had left, it came time and Jesus too went to Jerusalem (verse 10).

During this part of His ministry Jesus taught rather freely in the Temple, "and no one laid hands on Him, for His hour had not yet come" (John 8:20). But when He instructed His disciples where to prepare for the Passover, He told them, "My time is at hand" (Matt. 26:18). And just prior to His betrayal and subsequent glorification, He again said with surety, "The hour has come" (John 17:1).

Before partaking of the Passover feast "Jesus knew that His hour had come that He should depart from this world to the Father" (John 13:1). When He later awoke the sleeping disciples in Gethsemane, He said, "The hour is at hand, and the Son of Man is being betrayed into the hands of sinners" (Matt. 26:45). There was also a set time for His resurrection. When the Jews asked Him for a sign, He said, "'Destroy this temple, and in three days I will raise it up.' . . . He was speaking of the temple of His body" (John 2:19-21).

Jesus' life and ministry were no haphazard improvisation. He followed a divinely planned schedule under the Spirit's constant guidance. As a result He was able to do the right thing in the right way at the right time. Such is the essence of righteousness within.

As humans we are often pressed and hampered by time and must occasionally postpone engagements. Unavoidably we have to delay projects because we cannot foresee or control circumstances. But not so with God. Both the originator and master of time, He sees all of it and controls it. Everything is under the ultimate mastery of the Infinite One. As the Creator and Ruler of the universe He is no helpless victim, as we humans at times tend to be. Being the master of time, He can fulfill His plans on divine schedule.

God does not relate to our planet in a helter-skelter fashion. Our world is no more a derelict ship in time than it is in space. All the planets, and the innumerable stars in God's universe, keep their steady course in both space and time. God is in control in both areas.

History is going somewhere. "Amidst the strife and tumult of nations, He that sitteth above the cherubim still guides the affairs of the earth. . . . God is overruling all for the accomplishment of His purposes."[4] "God's purposes know no haste and no delay."[5]

The whole creation moves toward one great event. And that is the second advent of Jesus to this earth. The time and season for it "the Father has fixed by His own authority" (Acts 1:7, RSV). He knows its time.

[1] Ellen G. White, *Patriarchs and Prophets*, p. 180.
[2] ————, *Prophets and Kings*, p. 700.
[3] ————, *The Desire of Ages*, p. 621.
[4] ————, *Education*, p. 178.
[5] ————, *The Desire of Ages*, p. 32.

CHAPTER 7

The Faithful Servant's Waiting

The Finnish track star Paavo Nurmi (1897-1973) never entered a race in a state of high excitement. But he was an undisputed champion during the 1920s, having won seven Olympic gold medals in races of 1 to 14 miles in length. "The Phantom Finn" planned every race precisely in relation to its distance and did not worry if other runners left him behind at the beginning of a long race. To gauge his speed, he always carried a stopwatch and knew how to pace himself.

We could compare Nurmi's way of running Olympic races to the manner the faithful and wise servant did his work (see Matt. 24:45, 46). Before the master left, he made him steward of his possessions with responsibility for seeing that all the other workers on the farm were well cared for and had what they needed. The servant filled an honorable position as his master's representative. Nevertheless he longed for his master's return.

Enjoying his work to the fullest when his master was at home with him, he constantly looked for his return, while at the same time faithfully attending to the duties his master had entrusted to him. While he did not know when his master would get back, that did not worry him. The servant had his work to do, and he did it with glad-hearted diligence, alertness, and moment-by-moment watchfulness, ever ready to welcome his master when he did show up.

The good servant did not let himself get overexcited or perform his work in a frenzy. No one could ever compare him to the seed that fell on stony places in the parable of the sower (Matt. 13:3-9). Initially the rocky soil appeared to be the best ground. Both moisture and warmth were ideal for quick germination and early growth. But because of the rocks the grain could not send down deep roots. And without deep roots it withered and died in the summer heat.

The seed that dropped on the good ground did not initially grow so fast and look so good, but it sank its roots deep into the soil. In this way it was able to endure the summer drought and produce up to a hundredfold yield.

The good-ground seed mirrors the faithful and wise servant. The grain sprouting on the good ground represents all the faithful and wise followers of Jesus. They are firmly founded on the Word and possess staying power for the long haul, not living in a fleeting daze of emotional excitement.

The faithful and wise Christian will run the Christian race the way Nurmi did his Olympic contests. "We are not to live upon time excitement," Ellen White advised.[1] Rather, the true Christian is calm and characterized by steady devotion to God's will and His work in sunny as well as in less pleasant days; and yet he or she is always alert for the Master's return.

Nothing will entice him away or divert him from his Christian commitment. He is not pessimistic, downhearted, and doubtful about his Master's coming even if the Master does not arrive back as soon as he had hoped. Nor does he ingeniously figure out or set a time for His return. Confidently leaving it up to his Master to decide as He sees best, the servant remembers that Jesus Himself told His disciples while on earth that not even He knew the time for His advent, but only His Father. And so he reasons, like the proverbial old farmer, that "God is always right on time."

Christ's teaching about the faithful and wise servant is that life must be a constant preparation for His coming. And the time before He returns should be one of joy, not fear. God's true servant will wait for the Second Advent as young Ellen Harmon did in 1844, with a heart "full of glad expectation." His anticipation will be like that of parents joyfully looking for their children to come home. Or like the bride waiting for the groom to arrive for the wedding.

A young woman told me on her wedding day that she had never been so happy as she had been since she met the man she was about to marry. The weeks and months she had spent looking forward to the marriage had been a time of sheer happiness. The waiting time of both parents and the bride-to-be are filled with happy preparation in anticipation of the joyous occasion. It is not squandered in idle daydreaming.

Luther once said, "If I knew the world was coming to an end tomorrow, I would still go out and plant three apple trees today." In other words, he would be doing just the work he thought was right and of lasting good value.

An African-American poet expressed the same sound philosophy of doing his work faithfully and well every day until Jesus returns, in the following lines:

> "There's a king and a captain high,
>   And he's coming by and by,
>   And he'll find me hoeing cotton when he comes.
>   You can hear his legions charging in the regions of the sky,
>   And he'll find me hoeing cotton when he comes.
>   There's a man they thrust aside,
>   Who was tortured till he died,
>   And he'll find me hoeing cotton when he comes.
>   He was hated and rejected,
>   He was scorned and crucified,
>   And he'll find me hoeing cotton when he comes.
>   When he comes! When he comes!
>   We'll be crowned by saints and angels when he comes.
>   They'll be shouting out Hosanna! to the man that men denied,
>   And I'll kneel among my cotton when he comes."[2]

Here we see depicted the attitude of the faithful and wise servant. The poem reflects and imitates the pattern set by Jesus Himself, who said, "My Father goes on working, and so do I" (John 5:17, Jerusalem).

Those who always keep on doing what they know they ought to do are happy, contented, and fearless. They realize that under the guidance of God's Word, and the promptings of the Holy Spirit, in harmony with the divine written instruction, they have done, are doing, and will do their duty to the best of their ability at all times. The apostle Paul had the same kind of peace of mind when he stood before the Sanhedrin at Claudius Lysias' order. "My conscience is perfectly clear about the way in which I have lived before God to this very day," he told them (Acts 23:1, TEV).

Such freedom before God and peace of conscience gave Paul invincible courage and stamina for effective service for God under the most forbidding circumstances. Inward peace enabled him to maintain emotional and mental sanity in the midst of extremely adverse experiences: "In labors more abundant, in stripes above measure, in prisons more frequently, in deaths often. From the Jews five times received I forty stripes minus one. Three times I was beaten with rods; once I was stoned; three times I was shipwrecked; a night and a day I have been in the deep; in journeys often, in perils of waters, in perils of robbers, in perils of my own countrymen, in perils of the Gentiles, in perils in the city, in perils in the wilderness, in perils in the sea, in perils among false brethren; in weariness and toil, in sleeplessness often, in hunger and thirst, in fastings often, in cold and nakedness—besides the other things, what comes upon me daily: my deep concern for all the churches" (2 Cor. 11:23-28). Such an outlook kept Paul ready and waiting for either death or the second advent of Jesus.

Sustained by loyal commitment to Jesus, the apostle could write when awaiting execution: "I have fought the good fight, I have finished the race, I have kept the faith. Finally, there is laid up for me the crown of righteousness, which the Lord, the righteous Judge, will give to me on that Day, and not to me only but also to all who have loved His appearing" (2 Tim. 4:7, 8).

Faithful servants will always demonstrate in their lives this counsel of Jesus to His disciples on the Mount of Olives: "Be careful not to let yourselves become occupied with too much feasting and drinking and with the worries [cares] of this life, or that Day may suddenly catch you like a trap" (Luke 21:34, 35, TEV).

And faithful servants will let nothing turn them from their task of serving their Master loyally at all times. Patiently they will wait while God works out His plan according to His divine time schedule, rather than trying to impose theirs on Him. To do the latter is to imply that their Master is dilatory when His actions do not conform to their own cherished ideas.

We can accurately measure the depth of a person's conviction by its impact upon the individual's life—his or her aims, plans, work, and stewardship of means, time, and personal physical strength and mental ability. A young professional once confided to me that he followed one standard in acquiring, using, and keeping his means and in using time: "Will this help or hinder me in being ready for the second coming of Jesus?" I believe that is a good gauge for measuring one's use of both time and possessions.

A Christian's belief in the nearness of the Second Advent will inevitably affect what that individual says and does today. If, on the other hand, it has no visible effect on his or her life and daily actions, a Christian's profession may consist only of words. And words are often cheap. Easily spoken, they cost nothing without actual investment in deeds.

If we are indeed good servants and genuine followers of Jesus, we will follow the example of our Master, who declared, "I must work the works of Him who sent Me while it is day; the night is coming when no one can work" (John 9:4).

In the parable of the pounds, the servants whom the master commended on his return were those who had kept busy trading with the capital he had entrusted to them. They had not waited in idleness. Actively engaged in the work their master had assigned them, they were prepared for his return at any moment. Not one of them was sitting at his desk trying to figure out when the master would arrive.

The Bible histories of Joseph, Ruth, Esther, Daniel, and others demonstrate how God wants us to act in normal circumstances as well as in times of subtle temptation and crisis. Instead of rushing about in euphoric frenzy that renders us unable to attend to the daily tasks of everyday life, we will—like these heroes and heroines of genuine faith—steadfastly attend to our daily duties. Such biblical men and women show us how to translate our love for God into concrete form. Their love for God enabled them to overcome the strongest temptations to sensuous pleasure, and even the fear of death itself.

The master did not come as soon as the servants had hoped or expected. But it neither disturbed nor unsettled the faithful and wise servant. A genuine adventist, he maintained his trust in his master, even though he would have liked him to return sooner.

We are Seventh-day Adventists. As such, we live to the full in the present in light of the future—as did the faithful and wise servant in Jesus' parable—yearningly watching for Christ's coming. In this way we will hail our Lord's return with joy whether it will be while we are still alive or at our resurrection (see 1 Thess. 4:16, 17). Our joy will abound as we receive our reward of being made rulers "over all his goods" (Matt. 24:47)—a stark contrast to the evil servant's fate, as we will see in the next chapter.

---

[1] Ellen G. White, *Selected Messages*, book 1, p. 189.

[2] Quoted in William Barclay, ed. and tr., *The Gospel of Matthew*, rev. ed. (Philadelphia: Westminster Press, 1975), vol. 2, p. 318.

CHAPTER 8

The Evil Servant's Waiting

Once one of my students was not doing well in my class, so I visited him to find out his problem. When I asked him if he had enough time to study, he replied, "Oh, yes."

"Do you have a job on campus, or do you work somewhere else?" I continued.

"Oh, no, I don't work."

Since he had no job or afternoon labs, I inquired what he did in the afternoons. "Oh, I go out to the gym and shoot a few hoops."

Study was never uppermost in his mind. Because he knew he had an abundance of time, he always felt at ease postponing his study.

William Barclay once commented that "the Second Coming of Jesus is a doctrine which has to a large extent dropped out of Christian thinking and preaching. The curious thing about it is that the Christians seem either entirely to disregard it or to think of nothing else."[1]

My student felt no urgency to study during the afternoon. He knew he had the whole evening free for study, plus his free hours the next forenoon. So he dismissed the thought of study for the present and always deferred it to the future. After all, he always felt he had plenty of time. And it led to educational disaster.

The evil servant in Christ's parable (see Matt. 24:48-51) did not scoff at the idea of his master's return. He believed just as firmly in it as did the faithful and wise servant. But inasmuch as his master did not arrive as soon as he had expected, he concluded that his master "will not come back for a long time" (verse 48, TEV). He assumed that he had ample time to get ready for his master's appearance.

The evil servant thought and acted as my delinquent student did. Since the servant assumed he had ample time, he saw no need to be ready, nor even to prepare. So he banished the thought of his master's return from his mind. Instead he followed his own inclinations and did what most appealed to him, as my student did. The servant decided to taste all the alluring pleasures of the world. After he had done that, he then planned to turn his will and attention to doing his master's business, and thus prepare for his coming. Never for a moment did it occur to him that his master might show up suddenly and unexpectedly.

The servant's reasoning gradually lead him to lapse into careless living, and he began to "drink with the drunkards" (verse 49). Jesus warned against this very mode of waiting when he cautioned, "Be on guard so that your hearts are not weighed down with dissipation and drunkenness and the worries of this life, and that day catch you unexpectedly, like a trap" (Luke 21:34, 35, NRSV).

A trap always suddenly and unexpectedly catches its prey. So Jesus admonished, "Therefore you also must be ready, for the Son of Man is coming at an unexpected hour" (Matt. 24:44, NRSV).

But having started to indulge in sensuous pleasures, the evil servant did not stop at that. His sensitivity to wrongdoing dulled, he began to mistreat and hurt his fellow servants. He became so cruel and hard-hearted to those whose welfare the master had entrusted to him that he began "to beat his fellow servants" (verse 49), smiting them with accusations and condemnations. The inevitable result of his disloyalty to his master was transformation into an evil servant.

But there are other unfaithful servants besides the perennial evildoers. On the surface these others may not seem so disgusting.

They are not necessarily extravagant and dissolute in their pursuits of pleasure. Instead they are just postponing current duties, like my former student was.

The mañana, or tomorrow, syndrome will lead to spiritual disaster. After being stirred by the Holy Spirit to commit his life to God, Felix, the Roman governor of Judea and Samaria, said to Paul, "Go away for now; when I have a convenient time I will call for you" (Acts 24:25). For Felix "a convenient time" never came.

The best time to respond to God's call is now. *Now* is the most important moment in any person's life. The Holy Spirit admonishes us, "Behold, now is the accepted time; behold, now is the day of salvation" (2 Cor. 6:2). The Germans have summed up the thought in a cogent saying that translated runs like this: "What you can do today, don't postpone until tomorrow."

The tempter does not usually suggest to a Christian that he abandon his allegiance to God. Rather Satan whispers that there is still plenty of time so that the person can do what he himself really enjoys, and then after that he can turn to God and His service. One of the most effective temptations imaginable, it is also a most dangerous delusion.

One group of Christians, mentioned by Barclay in the quote earlier in this chapter, think of nothing else but the Second Advent. Always gazing wistfully toward heaven, they are single-track-minded dreamers so engrossed in thinking of Christ's heavenly coming that they are of no earthly good. They are like a car with its engine running at high speed while the wheels dig themselves ever deeper into the mud. Frenetically active, they accomplish nothing. And inevitably their fervor will fade. In a sense they are one breed of "rocky ground" believers (Matt. 13:5, NRSV).

The apostle Paul spoke of his Jewish kinsfolk as having "a zeal for God, but not according to knowledge" (Rom. 10:2). They meticulously observed the multiplied rules of the rabbis. "The 10,000 legal definitions and decisions, which are now comprised in religious jurisprudence, were for the most part elaborated in those years [the time of Jesus], and every devout Israelite made it the labor of his life to observe them faithfully, as far as possible."[2] In this way they became evil servants.

The evil servant's mind and interests were not in tune with those of his master. Rather, his own interests took precedence. Every organization has members whose principles do not harmonize with its objectives. They have joined just because of personal benefits. Many of them are worldly wise and progressive and reach high positions. Judas was one example. Just as he did, they often became leaders—in the same manner as goats function as leaders of the sheep under the direction of the shepherd.

Most of the men who worked under Noah in building the ark did not share his sense of mission. They had no appreciation of the ark's purpose and destiny. Nevertheless they did good work, and for that they earned good wages.

The evil servant chose not to rearrange his thinking so as to make room for the outworking of his master's plans in his life. His own inclinations had priority in the apportionment of both his time and means.

Erroneously, the evil servant indulged the notion that he could gain the world and still be prepared for eternal fellowship with his master. He fancied he could have the best of both—a fatal notion that both prompted his actions and shaped his character. Because of his unfaithfulness in his stewardship, he lost the capital initially entrusted to him and he himself was cast "into outer darkness" (Matt. 25:30; cf. Luke 19:20-27). The evil servant portrays the end of every disloyal follower of God.

---

[1] William Barclay, ed. and tr., *The Gospel of John*, rev. ed., (Philadelphia: Westminster Press, 1975), vol. 2, p. 155.

[2] Cunningham Geike, *The Life and Words of Christ*, vol. 1, p. 176.

CHAPTER 9

Just Weary of Waiting

It is not uncommon that the faith of even God's committed followers staggers at times. We see it happen particularly when the fulfillment of His promises is a long time in coming. Abraham is one example.

The apostle Paul called Abraham "the father of all who believe" (Rom. 4:11, NIV). But before he matured in faith, Abraham's trust in God collapsed at times. Twice in foreign countries his faith failed him. Fearing for his life, he prevailed upon Sarah to tell people that he was her brother rather than her husband (see Gen. 12:10-20; 20:1-16). It was a half truth, since Sarah was indeed the daughter of his father but not of Abraham's mother. But in the sight of God it was a gross untruth because Abraham intended it to deceive. Then despairing of seeing God's promise of a son fulfilled through Sarah, he took Hagar to help him actualize God's promise (see Gen. 16:1-4).

David's faith also wavered. At the direct command of God Samuel anointed him to become king of Israel. And David accepted the divine promise. But instead of achieving kingship, he soon found himself chased as a wild beast by an emotionally disturbed king. When his life as a fugitive stretched into a decade, doubt and unbelief invaded and finally took possession of his heart. From having been a Goliath in faith with complete trust in God and His help, David shrank into a God-fearing dwarf.

As a result of his abandonment of faith in God's promise, David allied himself with the Philistines to find security. For a second time he turned to King Achish of Gath, this time pretending to be his loyal supporter (see 1 Sam. 27:1-28:2). He posed as an enemy of those "he afterward would be called upon to rule when God's appointed time should come," as Ellen White phrased it.[1] God's time for David's ascent to the throne of Israel had not yet arrived. The adverse experiences that befell him God intended as divine preparation for his kingship.

Many former Advent believers have been overwhelmed with deep sorrow that Jesus has not yet returned. But constant sorrow often breeds doubt. And doubt easily slips into total disbelief and even cynicism, leading to rejection of God. Some who once believed in Christ's soon return have tragically lost hope in the reality of His Second Advent. They have become scoffers, making light of the very thought of His second advent that they once so ardently espoused.

Others who have waited perhaps for a lifetime for the Second Advent have become disillusioned. They have heard the cry "Wolf, wolf!" so long that they doubt the very existence of a wolf. Such individuals have suffered eschatological burnout. Some who once fervently believed it would happen speedily now feel that they have been deceived by the message of His soon coming. To them the proclamation of the Second Advent has proved to be a hoax, and they may turn away from it with disgust. The consequence is often rejection of all religion and joining the enemies of God, as David temporarily did.

Many of us in the Seventh-day Adventist Church grew up in homes permeated with the belief that Jesus would soon come. Some of us have heard that thought expressed since we were small. We hardly expected to reach maturity and certainly did not expect to encounter old age. Having assumed that Jesus would come before we died, we now find ourselves getting elderly. Our contemporaries are dying off one by one.

As it happens, for some the God of their childhood is also dying. They really wonder whether God has deceived them or whether He really exists. The reason for their loss of faith in God is that—to them—He is not behaving as they expected Him to.

Unfortunately, a number of Seventh-day Adventists have also figured out ingenious timetables for end-time events that set a definite schedule for the Second Advent. They think they have captured God by their time charts. When God refuses to comply with their scenarios, they may lose faith in Him.

Other Seventh-day Adventists have developed the mental state of the Old Testament Jews. In Ezekiel's day the promise of the Messiah had been repeated for more than 3,000 years, and yet He had not come. Century after century had crept by. The disappointment and frustration had resulted in disbelief in all prophecy and crystallized into the proverb: "The days go by and every vision comes to nothing" (Eze. 12:22, NIV). By the time Jesus was born, faith in the Messiah had grown dim, and "hope had well-nigh ceased to illuminate the future." [2]

Some Seventh-day Adventists often speak of their disappointment that the second advent of Christ has been so long in coming. Almost embarrassed about our Advent belief, a number find themselves being pushed into disbelief. The alleged delay of Christ's parousia has made others feel like spiritual orphans or that they have been abandoned. They fear the lapse of time has made them look like losers. It seems that the longer time lasts, the less credible they and their Advent message becomes.

As a result, uncertainty regarding the Second Advent plagues many Seventh-day Adventists today. The zealous commitment to the Advent message has tapered off. The sense of mission of our forebears has been diluted or even vanished among many. And consequently it is not transmitted to our children and youth growing up in Adventist homes.

Parallel reactions to the failed hope of seeing Jesus' return also occurred among the Adventists who had looked longingly and expectantly for Jesus to arrive on October 22, 1844.

The faith of many of the 50,000 to 100,000 Advent believers faltered after the October disappointment. It had not been anchored in an intimate and loving fellowship with God through the indwelling of the Holy Spirit. As it crumbled under the onslaught of bafflement and blighted hope, it culminated in doubt and rejection of both the Advent message and God. Many Millerites suffered the fate of David, the fugitive from King Saul. Unfortunately, that is the experience of some Seventh-day Adventists even today.

Why do some believers lose faith and get discouraged or disillusioned when they do not see their hopes fulfilled as quickly as they expected, while the faith of others remains strong? Ellen White, speaking of some who renounced their faith after the 1844 disappointment, said of them in the language of the parable that they "'took their lamps, and took no oil with them.' They had moved from impulse. Their fears had been excited by the solemn message, but they had depended upon the faith of their brethren, satisfied with the flickering light of good emotions, without a thorough understanding of the truth or a genuine work of grace in the heart. These had gone forth to meet the Lord, full of hope in the prospect of immediate reward; but they were not prepared for delay and disappointment. When trials came, their faith failed, and their lights burned dim."[3]

All the bridesmaids in the parable had the correct belief. In a sense they were credible and "good" Seventh-day Adventists. But the five foolish bridesmaids were strangers to the Holy Spirit. They mistook conformity for conversion. Some had undoubtedly experienced conversion, but the new life within had been aborted. The Holy Spirit had not become a permanent, daily houseguest within to revitalize and guide them.

Such members are found in today's Seventh-day Adventist Church. They count themselves as genuine believers and associate with God's true people represented by the other five virgins. Most of their friends are within the Seventh-day Adventist Church. They even love to hear the gospel preached. But they are not acquainted with the Spirit. And God does not recognize them as His own, even though they have been working faithfully in the church (cf. Matt. 7:21-23).

It is encouraging and comfortable when we understand something. But our faith in God must not consist solely in understanding God's will and ways. Even more important is personal fellowship with God and glad-hearted willingness to follow His biddings to the extent of one's comprehension.

May God-trusting Abraham and David become our role models. Abraham, after having wavered in faith, became "the friend of God" (James 2:23) and "the father of all who believe" (Rom. 4:11, NIV). And David, after earlier joining God's enemies because of a lack of trust in Him, was transformed by divine molding power into "a man after [God's] own heart" (Acts 13:22). May those who today waver in faith—and might even have joined the enemies of God, as did David when he allied himself with King Achish of Gath—come back and even become leaders of God's people, as did Abraham and David.

When together we grow and mature to the spiritual stature where we trust God as little children do even when they do not understand, then we will become faithful and wise stewards. Then we will serve the Lord our God "with joy and gladness of heart" (Deut. 28:47) until He comes, not in keeping with our speculative timetables, but at His appointed time. Maranatha!

---

[1] Ellen G. White, in *Signs of the Times*, Nov. 9, 1888.

[2] ———, *The Desire of Ages*, p. 32.

[3] ———, *The Great Controversy*, p. 394.

CHAPTER 10

God Too Is Waiting

We noted in chapter 5 that God is enthroned above time. As such He can now or already see His followers "sit together in heavenly places in Christ Jesus" (Eph. 2:6).

But God also shares the feelings of His Son while on earth and humans in looking forward to or waiting for the moment when His earthborn children will share *His* "now or already." Jesus told the disciples, "'In the regeneration, when the Son of Man sits on the throne of His glory, you who have followed Me will also sit on twelve thrones'" (Matt. 19:28; cf. Matt. 26:29; John 14:2, 3).

God the Father is the great Lover. He looks forward to the moment when sweet fellowship and the poignant hush of the intimate communion of lovers will replace the sin-caused broken relationship between Him and His human children. The prophet Zephaniah depicts this union. "'Do not fear; Zion, let not your hands be weak. The Lord your God in your midst, the Mighty One, will save; He will rejoice over you with gladness, He will quiet you in His love, He will rejoice over you with singing'" (Zeph. 3:16, 17).

God's joy will then be complete. But for the moment He still waits.

All humans—men, women, and children—know what it means to wait. Everyone has experienced it, whether healthy or sick, free or imprisoned, rich or poor.

Children wait for birthdays and holidays. They wait for the time that they will be old enough to go to school. Once in school, they anticipate finishing grade school so that they can begin high school. Even then the waiting is not over. It begins all over again. Those who have finished their education look forward to finding a congenial job. Having obtained one, some unfortunately begin to wait for the weekend, vacation, or the day they can retire.

Sick patients wait for the time when they will be well again. Individuals in prison anticipate their eventual release. Even those on death row wait. They wait for a pardon—or execution.

As a teacher I have often waited for the final examinations. The students too have waited for them and for the end of the semester and possible graduation. Such waiting begins as soon as the course begins. Both I and my students knew from the beginning of the term when the final examination would come. Nevertheless, we waited for it together.

That students always eagerly wait for graduation from their different educational programs does not mean that anything has postponed their graduations. They know the time for their graduations from the beginning. Nevertheless, they wait for them with keen anticipation. The parents, spouses, and friends of the students also wait with them.

Parents—especially retired parents who are not so preoccupied with a workaday life—always eagerly wait for the children to come home for a visit.

Without a doubt God is also more eager to welcome His human children home than we may be to leave earth and go home to heaven. One reason for this might be that some people look upon heaven as depriving them of doing something they now enjoy.

A minister of the gospel one day entered a bar in search of converts. He went up to a customer seated at the bar and said, "Do you want to go to heaven?"

The man with a glass of beer in his hand answered, "I sure do."

Approaching the next person, the clergyman asked him the same question. The response was just as affirmative. The third man also expressed his desire to go to heaven. The minister was glad. So far everyone wanted to go to heaven.

But when the minister reached the fourth customer, he received the unexpected reply, "No, I don't!"

Puzzled, the clergyman said, "So you mean you don't want to go to heaven when you die?"

"Oh, yes, I sure want to go to heaven when I die," the drinking man answered eagerly, "but I thought you were making up a group right now."

Some people, engaged in things they really enjoy, do not like to be interrupted, not even by going to be with Jesus and God in heaven. Others, like some young people, would like to get married first.

But heaven will not frustrate anyone's hope for total fulfillment. It will rob no one of the realization of his or her best dreams and desires. Unfortunately, many do not believe that. The return of Jesus is not an interruption or cancellation of anything good in the present life. It is rather the eternal extension and fulfillment of something better—something more wonderful than anything anyone has ever experienced or even been able to imagine.

Parents wait for their children to come home because they love them. God loves His children even more deeply than human parents. Therefore He suffers infinitely more acutely when separated from His children. Imagine the pain of a father and mother allowed to see their child only at a long distance. This is God's present relationship to His earth children.

He has not been with His children face-to-face since Adam and Eve left the Garden of Eden. It is not because He does not want to, but because they are now contaminated by sin and to them He would be a "consuming fire" (Heb. 12:29). When Jesus, or Emmanuel—"God with us" (Matt. 1:23)—came to earth to redeem us, He had to veil His glory lest it strike men and women dead.

God is fervently looking forward to the great family reunion in heaven. Then Jesus will again drink the Communion wine with all the redeemed. At "the marriage supper of the Lamb" (Rev. 19:9)

Jesus will share it with the redeemed to celebrate the restoration of eternal face-to-face communion with "nothing between" His brothers and sisters. And His Father Himself will be there, rejoicing, that all His redeemed earth children—among them Adam and Eve—"shall see His face, and His name shall be on their foreheads" (Rev. 22:4). God longs and waits for this grand family reunion.

As the festivities of the marriage reception inaugurate the intimate togetherness of the married couple, so the Lamb's wedding feast introduces God's eternal personal fellowship with the redeemed. The Bible repeatedly uses the marriage relationship to symbolize the deep relationship that exists between the genuine believer and God. The Song of Solomon pictures this loving marriage relationship. The whole book is a collection of love poems spoken alternately by a lover and his beloved. In a spiritual sense the lover is Jesus, and the object of His love is the individual believer, or collectively, the church.

We find the central theme of the Song of Solomon epitomized in 2:16, where the woman exclaims, "My beloved is mine, and I am his." Verse three of chapter 6 echoes the same sentiment: "I am my beloved's, and my beloved is mine." It comes back a third time in 7:10: "I am my beloved's, and his desire is toward me."

God's desire has always been toward every person born into the world. No one is his or her own—including you and me. God's creative power brought us into existence. By creation we belong to Him. And when we were lost in sin He redeemed us by His blood. So we are twice His. We belong to the heavenly Bridegroom. The apostle Paul reminded his readers, "And you are Christ's" (1 Cor. 3:23). By all rights we are totally His.

It was His love for us that evoked our love for Him. "We love Him because He first loved us," the apostle said in 1 John 4:19. A suitor's love for a woman usually arouses her love for him. Such is our relationship to Jesus. We give ourselves to Him because He first gave Himself to us. It evokes mutual attachment and devotion in a surrender like that of a married couple giving themselves to each other. The Holy Spirit leads believers to intimate communion with their God—a communion that will be celebrated and cemented for eternity at the heavenly family reunion soon to come. God is longing and waiting for it to begin.

It is a joy to go to a family reunion or even a class reunion. Just as we look forward to them, so God, our Father, and Jesus, our Elder Brother, and the Holy Spirit eagerly anticipate this first family reunion with all the redeemed. God is waiting for togetherness in harmony and joy.

The fact that parents continuously wait for their children to come home does not imply that anything has delayed or postponed the visit. Their love and interest for and in their children make them wait for them all the time. Incessantly. They miss them and wish they would stop by more often.

In the same way, the Father and Jesus are waiting for us earth children to come home. Not just for a visit, but to stay forever.

Jesus and His Father are longing for you and me. They are waiting for us to leave our sin-sick earth to join Them in Their heavenly home—a home beyond sorrow, suffering, pain, trials, adversity, and even death.

God is patiently waiting. Waiting in order to give every person ample time to make a deliberate and definite decision whether or not he or she wants to be with Jesus and His Father for eternity. As Peter said: "The Lord is not slack concerning His promise [of Christ's second advent], as some count slackness, but is longsuffering toward us, not willing that any should perish but that all should come to repentance" (2 Peter 3:9). Heaven is waiting for earth's spiritual harvest.

CHAPTER 11

The Harvesttime

Jesus told His disciples that "the harvest is the end of the world" (Matt. 13:39, KJV). When the spiritual harvest is ripe—both wheat and tares—or when everyone has settled into truth or made an irreversible decision against Jesus, then Jesus will return.

Just before earth's harvest the revelator pictures Christ as sitting on a white cloud holding a sharp sickle in His hand. An angel then calls out from the heavenly temple, "Thrust in Your sickle and reap, for the time has come for You to reap, for the harvest of the earth is ripe" (Rev. 14:15).

The question then immediately arises: "What determines the ripening of the harvest?"

We know there will be no harvest without planting or seeding. During our two years on the wheat plains of North Dakota we observed how farmers seeded their fields in the spring. After having completed it in the best way at the right time, they then patiently waited for the crops to grow and mature. At times they might spray their fields with insecticides.

The ripening of the grain hinges on the season and the weather. Depending on the rain, the temperature, and the sun, some years the grain grows faster and matures earlier than others. But the farmer has no control over such factors. They are ultimately in the hands of God, although Satan often manipulates them.

The apostle Paul calls Satan "the ruler of the kingdom of the air" (Eph. 2:2, NIV). The apostle John goes so far as to say that "the whole world is under the control of the evil one" (1 John 5:19, NIV). Jesus Himself called the evil one "the ruler of this world" (John 12:31; 14:30; 16:11). The apostle Paul, like his Lord, did not want his followers to underestimate the power of the one whom he even called "the god of this age" (2 Cor. 4:4).

The book of Job gives a graphic illustration of Satan's intrusive destruction. The devil doubted Job's moral integrity and challenged God by inferring that the patriarch served Him only for selfish reasons. To disprove Satan's insinuations, the Lord granted the devil the right to test Job. Instantly Satan afflicted Job through two weather calamities: "The fire of God fell from heaven" (Job 1:16; in typical Hebrew fashion the author attributes the fire to God even though Satan obviously was behind it) and "a great wind came from across the wilderness" (verse 19), causing the death of all Job's children. In addition, two other disasters engineered by men but prompted by Satan befell Job—the theft of his livestock and the murder of their herdsmen (see verses 14, 15, 17). Satan is a terrible enemy of God's creation. The apostle Paul said that "the whole creation groans and labors with birth pangs together" (Rom. 8:22) under his cruel management.

The authority of both Satan and evil persons stems from God's creation of them as free-willed moral beings, something He did deliberately because He longed for fellowship with beings somewhat like Himself, that is, able to make free moral choices. He hoped that they would choose to stay within the bounds of His will, a desire He expressed to Adam and Eve. "Of every tree of the garden you may freely eat; but of the tree of knowledge of good and evil you shall not eat, for in the day that you eat of it you shall surely die" (Gen. 2:16, 17).

Even after they had chosen to go against His will, God still granted them an area in which to operate. Satan—who originated sin, or departure from God's will—also has a definite sphere of influence and power. Our world itself suffers from his power and yearns for deliverance, as Paul so graphically mentioned (Rom. 8:20-22).

Being aware of Satan's malicious intent particularly against His loyal followers, God made provision for their safety. He built a fence of protection around His people. Satan challenged God that His servant Job served Him only from selfish reasons because of His protection within His hedge (see Job 1:10). To show Satan Job's integrity, God granted the evil one special permission to intrude beyond that boundary and hurt Job.

As His people Israel waited to enter the Promised Land, God told them He would control the weather for their safety and good. Canaan, He said, was not like Egypt, "where you lived before. There, when you planted grain, you had to work hard to irrigate the fields; but the land you are about to enter . . . is a land watered by rain. The Lord your God takes care of this land and watches over it throughout the year. . . . He will send rain on your land when it is needed, in the autumn and in the spring, so that there will be grain, wine, and olive oil for you, and grass for your cattle. You will have all the food you want" (Deut. 11:10-15, TEV).

The climate of Palestine would be dependable under God's direction. He would see to it that their crops would ripen on time. Thus it was His responsibility, not that of the Israelite farmers or of the crops themselves. As God ordered the weather for the obedient Israelites so that the barley harvest would come at the right time, so He will also direct conditions so that earth's spiritual harvest will ripen at the right moment.

The earth's spiritual harvest occurs at the Second Advent. God's church, like the farmer, has to sow the seed at the right time, in the right way. We—the church—are responsible for planting the gospel seed.

But praise the Lord for modern technological inventions. National borders do not stop radio waves and TV pictures. Not even the iron curtain of Eastern Europe was completely able to insulate its people from the messages and pictures of freedom coming from the West. Nor can the bamboo curtain of the Far East do that.

But even when we do our best, our efforts do not determine the time for earth's harvest and Christ's return. Like the ripening of the grain on the wheat fields of America, so the maturing of the earth's spiritual harvest depends primarily on forces outside of human control.

Our world, though invaded and pervaded by sin, is not the victim of the mindless or whimsical decisions and actions of a rebel race under the ultimate authority of Satan. The rebels and their leader can affect conditions and circumstances, but they do not control earth's destiny nor God's eternal plan for it. God is the Lord of the universe, and also the earth's ultimate ruler and the Lord of time.

According to the fulfilled time prophecies, we now live in the season for the maturing of the grain and the second advent of Christ, the Great Harvester. Although the farmers know the season for the ripening of the grain, they do not know exactly the date and day they will be able to begin the harvest.

God is different from us. Never the victim of uncertainty, He knows the machinations of the evil one, and He will order the spiritual climate for the ripening of the earth's spiritual harvest just as He controlled the climate of ancient Canaan for the ripening of Israel's wheat harvest. Besides, He sees the end from the beginning. God foresaw both the planting of the seed and the time for the harvest. On the basis of His foreknowledge He knew and planned when best it should happen.

"The Big Dry"[1] during the summer of 1988, with its record temperatures, illustrates how climate affects the ripening of the harvest. It brought in the forest fire season two months early in the mountain states and along the West Coast. In addition it also ripened the peaches and apricots, among other fruits, more than a month early in southern California. The fruit harvest ended long before it should have.

So we as spiritual farmers will plant the seed of truth but leave it to God to make it ready for the spiritual harvest of souls for His kingdom. "The growth and perfection of the seed rests not with the husbandman. God alone can ripen the harvest. But man's cooperation is required."[2]

God controls the time for the ripening of the wheat on the vast wheat fields of Western United States. In the same way earth's spiritual harvest and the time for Christ's Second Advent are not determined by man, but rest in God's trustworthy hands.

---

[1] "The Big Dry," *Time*, July 4, 1988, pp. 12-17.
[2] Ellen G. White, *Testimonies to Ministers*, p. 508.

CHAPTER 12

Can Humans Hasten the Harvest?

Let us suppose that one year a certain farmer, for what he considers good reasons, would like to get his wheat harvest finished early. He has something else exceptionally important to do during the usual harvest season. Filled with eagerness to get the crops in ahead of schedule, he wonders if there's something he might do to hasten the ripening of his wheat. But there is really not much he can do. God Himself through the apostle Paul gives the categorical answer: "So then neither he who plants is anything, nor he who waters, but God who gives the increase" (1 Cor. 3:7). The ripening of the grain simply does not depend on the farmer.

Unlike the farmer, God controls the climate as well as the circumstances that will bring earth's spiritual harvest to fruition. As we said in the previous chapter, God is the master of earth's spiritual harvest.

As the farmer has people working with and for him, so God has enlisted His followers to labor with Him in the harvest. Thus we do have a responsibility in bringing it in—or rather a privilege of aid-ing God in finishing His work. But that does not mean that the success of His plans rests on us.

In a certain business enterprise one employee fills a pivotal position. But if that employee fails in that position, that does not mean that the employer is at his or her mercy. The business owner simply resorts to other means or moves another person into the position to insure the continued success of the enterprise. So it is with God. And His resources are limitless. He has a thousand ways to provide for any possible emergency.

If we, as His people, are unwilling, He will find other means to present His last-day message. During His triumphal entry into Jerusalem the Pharisees wanted Jesus to quiet the people who acclaimed Him as "the King who comes in the name of the Lord!" "But He answered and said to them, 'I tell you that if these should keep silent, the stones would immediately cry out'" (Luke 19:38, 40). If men and women refuse, children—and even stones and rocks—will proclaim His last message to the world.

God has used children before. During the Advent awakening in Europe (1830-1845) the law prohibited anyone but ministers of the state church to preach in Sweden. Some who tried, like Ole Boqvist and Erik Walbom, the authorities sent to prison. As a result the child preachers of Sweden arose to proclaim God's message for the hour.[1] If need be, God will do the same again. Or the stones will cry out.

At times I am afraid we as a church speak too much about *our* finishing God's mission on earth. The task of sounding the gospel invitation is ultimately God's work, not ours. But He longs to have us join Him in it.

Undoubtedly God must smile many a time when He hears us innocently speak about "finishing the work." The expression reminds me of the ready and willing help our oldest daughter offered me when she was just 4 years old. I have forgotten what my wife, Mae, and I were discussing at the time. We wanted to buy something, and I said we did not have the money. Little Karen, hearing of our need, suddenly disappeared. In a few moments she returned with her little piggy bank. Offering it to me, she said, "Daddy, here. Take my money. Then you can buy it."

Lovable little Karen's attitude reflected her willingness to do all she could to help. Her desire to assist was indeed sweet and highly commendable, but as far as her monetary contribution was concerned, it really amounted to nothing.

Perhaps the incident illustrates our efforts in relation to finishing God's work on earth. The Lord loves our willingness to sacrifice and help. But that will never be effective in completing the evangelization of the world.

At times we almost give the impression that the gospel commission is solely our responsibility. But the task of giving the gospel to all the world is primarily God's work. While He eagerly desires our cooperation, never for a moment should we entertain the notion that we are indispensable. We assume too exalted an opinion of ourselves when we think He is utterly dependent on us. "God could have reached His object in saving sinners without our aid; but in order for us to develop a character like Christ's, we must share in His work."[2] "Those whom God employs as His messengers are not to feel that His work is dependent on them. Finite beings are not left to carry this burden of responsibility."[3]

"Many who profess to revere God . . . act as if God is under obligations to them, as if He cannot carry on His work without their aid. Let such gaze into the starry heavens, and with admiration and awe study the marvelous works of God."[4] If we procrastinate either in sowing the gospel seed or bringing in the harvest, "angels will do a work which men might have had the blessing of accomplishing, had they not neglected to answer the claims of God."[5]

We are not responsible for bringing the eschaton—the end of all things earthly. God will do that. Not we. "He will finish the work and cut it short in righteousness" (Rom. 9:28).

In the end-time God will fulfill the following promise: "The Holy Spirit, the representative of the Captain of the Lord's host, comes down to direct the battle. Our infirmities may be many, our sins and mistakes grievous; but the grace of God is for all who seek it with contrition. The power of Omnipotence is enlisted in behalf of those who trust in God."[6]

Under the direction of the Captain of the Lord's host, God's work on earth will come to completion in a blaze of glory. And the

Lord of the harvest shall not be compelled to resort to other means for finishing His work on earth. Psalm 110:3 assures us that when the Captain of the Lord's host musters His army for the final overthrow of the adversary and his followers, God's people will yield willing obedience to Him. Both young and old will then join Him with youthful vigor. God's people did that when Deborah vindicated the Lord before His ancient enemies (see Judges 5:2).

[1] L. E. Froom, *The Prophetic Faith of Our Fathers*, Vol. III, pp. 673-675.
[2] Ellen G. White, *The Desire of Ages*, p. 142.
[3] ———, *Prophets and Kings*, p. 176.
[4] ———, *Lift Him Up*, p. 54.
[5] ———, *Selected Messages*, book 1, p. 118.
[6] ———, *The Desire of Ages*, p. 352.

CHAPTER 13

The Ellen White Statement: "It Is in Our Power to Hasten Our Lord's Return"

Ellen White made such a statement in *The Desire of Ages* (first published in 1898). Using a marginal reading of the King James Version, she wrote, "By giving the gospel to the world it is in our power to hasten our Lord's return. We are not only to look for but to hasten the coming of the day of God. 2 Peter 3:12, margin." Then she continued: "Had the church of Christ done her appointed work as the Lord ordained, the whole world would before this have been warned, and the Lord Jesus would have come to our earth in power and great glory."[1]

"Hasting" in 2 Peter 3:12 rests on the Greek verb *speudoo* has two basic meanings: (1) hasten, and (2) hasten unto, or earnestly desire or earnestly long for. In other words, this Greek verb may be either transitive or intransitive. Most English versions of the Bible translate it "hasting" or use words or phrases with that meaning. They do the same in the other five places the New Testament employs the verb (Luke 2:16; 19:5, 6; Acts 20:16; 22:18).

Some modern English translations, however, follow the regular reading of the King James Version, which states "hasting unto the coming of the day of God." This rendering expresses desire or longing for the day of God, rather than the idea of speeding it up or making it come sooner. The American Standard Version, Phillips, and *The Jerusalem Bible* employ it, as do also *The Amplified Bible* and the New Revised Standard Version, the latter as an alternate reading.

The translation "earnestly desiring," or "earnestly longing [or long] for" brings the phrase into complete agreement with the preceding phrase "waiting for." In this case both verbs or action words in the verse describe the direction of the person's mind and emotions in expressing expectancy and desire. The believer properly couples intellectual anticipation with the heart's longing for the Lord's coming.

The verb *speudoo* also appears in Acts 20:16, as mentioned previously. Most English versions interpret the verse as saying that Paul "was hurrying to be at Jerusalem, if possible, on the Day of Pentecost." They indicate physical haste or that Paul was speeding up his travel. A few, however, translate it so as to express Paul's desire or longing to be in Jerusalem on the Day of Pentecost by using "hoped" (Phillips), "was anxious" (Jerusalem), and "was eager" (NEB, NRSV) instead of "was hurrying to be at Jerusalem."

It is interesting that Ellen White, in commenting on Paul's voyage to Jerusalem during his third missionary journey, deviates from most Bible translations of her day by writing on page 389 of *The Acts of the Apostles* that "Paul greatly desired to reach Jerusalem," rather than saying that he was hurrying to do so.

Here she used the intransitive meaning of the verb *speudoo*, expressing longing or desire, as does the regular reading of 2 Peter 3:12 in the King James Version, rather than the transitive marginal reading "hasting the coming" that she employed in *The Desire of Ages*. In September 1895, or shortly before she finished her manuscript for *The Desire of Ages*, she cited the same text at Cooranbong, Australia. This time she used the regular reading of KJV, in reprimanding some believers for not "hasting unto [desiring or longing for] the day of God"[2] rather than "hasting it" (transitive meaning).

In the *Review* of June 10, 1852, she had also cited 2 Peter 3:12 in speaking about professing Christians who should be "looking for and hasting unto the day of God," rather than "hasting it." In later publishing the major portion of her *Review* article in *Early Writings*, she used it exactly as the regular reading of the King James Version renders it: "'looking for the hasting unto [earnestly desiring] the coming of the day of God.' 2 Peter 3:11, 12."[3] She did the same in *The Acts of the Apostles*, page 536, and in *Testimonies to Ministers*, page 238.

It is interesting to note that in the same book, *The Acts of the Apostles*, only a few pages apart, Ellen White used 2 Peter 3:12 and gave the meaning "hastening unto the day of God," (or eagerly desiring and longing for the day of God) and also urged her fellow believers on page 600 "hasten the coming of the Saviour."

Apparently in using 2 Peter 3:12 in both ways Ellen White was not primarily concerned with time. She was, however, definitely eager to stir the flagging zeal of her fellow believers that they might be faithful and wise servants, deligently doing their Master's business while eagerly waiting for Him. On page 536 of *The Acts of The Apostles* she spoke of Peter's devotion to His Master and his dedication to faithful service while "hasting unto" or longing for the Lord's return. "To the tried and faithful ones the coming might seem long delayed, but the apostle assured them: 'The Lord is not slack concerning his promise, as some men count slackness; but is longsuffering to usward, not willing that any should perish, but that all should come to repentance.'"

Peter let the believers know that God was mercifully and patiently waiting so that everyone would have an opportunity deliberately and calmly to make a decision for or against salvation. And in the light of Christ's sure return, Peter challenged his fellow believers to be "looking for and hasting unto the coming of the day of God."

The purpose of her statement in *The Desire of Ages* about "hasting the coming of the day of God" seems to have the same intent. She wanted to arouse each believer to participate actively in the work their Master had entrusted to His followers.

Ellen White recognized that the progress of the gospel ultimately depends on God. "The power of man cannot hasten the work; with this must be united the power of heavenly intelligences. Only thus can the work of God be brought to perfection. Man cannot do God's part of the work. A Paul may plant, and an Apollos water, but God gives the increase."[4] Her statement reemphasizes that not even God's people can speed up His mission on earth apart from His active participation.

Would not God always be glad to help us when we endeavor to bring new members into the church by sharing our knowledge of His saving truth with them? It would seem so. But Ellen White revealed why conversions at times are few. "The reason that the Lord does not manifest His power more decidely is because there is so little spirituality among those who claim to believe the truth."[5]

And again: "The Lord does not now work to bring many souls into the truth, because of the church members who have never been converted and those who are once converted but who have backslidden."[6]

"Only the work accomplished with much prayer, and sanctified by the merit of Christ, will in the end prove to have been efficient for good."[7]

Ellen White affirmed that God ultimately is in control of His church and its task when she declared, "The program of coming events is in the hands of our Maker. The Majesty of heaven has the destiny of nations, as well as *the concerns of His church*, in His own charge."[8]

God's work on earth rests in His hands. He has power to hasten it if need be. And that is evidently what He will do in the end-time. "For He will finish the work and cut it short in righteousness, because the Lord will make a short work upon the earth" (Rom. 9:28).

But why has not Jesus yet returned in response to His followers' ardent longing? That is equivalent to asking, "Why did not the Messiah come earlier or sooner in Old Testament times?" The answer is that the advent of the Messiah occurred when the fullness of the time had come (Gal. 4:4) according to God's time schedule, not according to His people's expectations.

On the other hand, we can hasten the Second Advent in one way. When we are busy doing something interesting and enjoyable, time seems to fly. During long trips by plane or car, if you are animatedly visiting with someone, time flashes by. But if you just sit, doing nothing, time may drag. Living and working with vibrant faith in Christ's soon coming makes time pass swiftly. "Faith has power to make the distant near. It obliterates distance of time and space. But unbelief *reverses* the effect. It looks in at the wrong end of the telescope; it reduces realities to a mere speck. Unbelief corrupts all blessings; it makes sour the very cream of God's kindness."[9]

While Jacob served seven years for Rachel, every day he looked at her through eyes of love. As a result the seven years "seemed to him but a few days because of the love he had for her" (Gen. 29:20, NRSV). Looking forward to something we greatly desire seems to make time speed by.

But even though we may subjectively hasten the passage of time by being absorbed in our work, the *finishing of God's harvest* does not depend on us. Both the ripening of the harvest on the wheat fields of America and God's spiritual harvest on earth depend ultimately on Him, not on humans. "The Author of our salvation will be the Finisher of the work," Ellen White has assured us.[10]

---

[1] *The Desire of Ages*, p. 633, 634. In *Testimonies*, volume 8, page 22, and also in *The Acts of the Apostles*, page 600, she uses almost the identical statement, each followed by a condition.

[2] ———, *Testimonies to Ministers*, p. 238.

[3] ———, *Early Writings*, p. 108.

[4] ———, *Testimonies*, vol. 7, p. 298.

[5] ———, *Testimonies to Ministers*, p. 425.

[6] ———, *Testimonies*, vol. 6, p. 371.

[7] ———, *The Desire of Ages*, p. 362.

[8] ———, *Thoughts From the Mount of Blessing*, p. 121. (Italics supplied.)

[9] J. D. Davis, Homily on Ezekiel 12:21-28, in *Pulpit Commentary* (Grand Rapids; Eerdmans, 1975), vol. 12, p. 223.

[10] Ellen G. White, *Testimonies*, vol. 6, p. 449.

CHAPTER 14

Has God Postponed the Harvest and Christ's Second Coming?

Many honest followers of Christ have expressed the belief that God has delayed Christ's second advent, thus implying that He has postponed the time for the harvest. Believing that according to God's original plan Christ should have come already and the harvest long since gathered in, they reason that only God's postponement could have placed the Second Advent still in the future. And they feel that they find substantial evidence for such a position in the inspired writings of Ellen White.

Thinking back upon her and her fellow believers' experience in 1844, Ellen White wrote in 1883, "Had Adventists, after the great disappointment in 1844, held fast their faith, and followed on unitedly in the opening providence of God, receiving the message of the third angel and in the power of the Holy Spirit proclaiming it to the world, they would have seen the salvation of God, the Lord would have worked mightily with their efforts, the work would have been completed, and Christ would have come ere this to receive His people to their reward."[1]

Her statement may seem to suggest that Christ's return has been postponed. But that is not necessarily so. It is a conditional statement, although she does not specifically express its conditionality. Shortly after 1883 she included the statement in *The Spirit of Prophecy* and explicitly underlined its conditionality by introducing it with a conditional clause. From that time on, the sentiment appeared periodically in Ellen White's writings either with or without the stated conditionality.[2]

Many of us have reared children. As parents we have had the joy of having them work with us. When they grew older we assigned them tasks to perform on their own. In giving a child work, perceptive parents allow time for procrastination since most children will by nature dillydally. After a while we would always check on their progress. Usually they had done well, but the job would not be entirely finished. Then we might have said, "You have done a good job, son, but if you had worked diligently all the time, you could have been through by now."

Our children had not completed their tasks as soon as they might have because they had not consistently applied themselves to their tasks—other interests had sidetracked their attention.

Many of us grown-ups also are procrastinators, and so are God's children. As parents know that their children put off things, so God knew and knows that many of His children postpone responsibilities. He foresaw this and even the exact extent of their dilatoriness at the very beginning of the detour of sin, and He made adjustment for it in His plan. For God, that was simple, since He sees the end from the beginning. Today's English Version expresses God's awareness of people's future doings in this way: "From the beginning I predicted the outcome; long ago I foretold what would happen" (Isa. 46:10).

The nonfulfillment of the condition in the nineteenth century presented no surprise to God. He already knew that the Sundaykeeping Adventists of 1844 would not become Seventh-day Adventists and help herald the three angels' messages. The Lord also foresaw the slowness of the early Seventh-day Adventists to grasp God's plan for them to evangelize the world.

Ellen White's conditional statements are comparable to saying that if humanity had not sinned, Jesus would not have had to come to our world and experience the Incarnation in order to redeem us. But God knew that sin would occur and that His incarnate Son would become humanity's Redeemer.

Likewise God already knew that Christ's second advent would not occur when it might have happened had people reacted differently to His expressed will and made different decisions leading to different behavior and actions. Since God foresaw all contingencies—all the varied choices men and women make—He made due allowances for them in His plan for the Second Advent.

Many have the impression that the moment for the Second Advent is fluid, or that it depends upon how soon the remnant church finishes the task of giving the gospel to the whole world. If that were indeed the case, Jesus might have answered the disciples' anxious query about the time of His return something like this: "My Father has not yet decided the time for My return. That decision is still left open in My Father's plan. It just depends on you and how you and your successors get along in fulfilling the gospel commission I gave you, and of your developing characters like Mine."

His response was nothing like that, however. Although as a man Jesus did not know the date for His Second Coming, He affirmed to the disciples that that time "the Father has fixed by His own authority" (Acts 1:7, RSV). As the moment for Christ's first advent rested on an established date in God's plan for our planet, so does also His second advent. That poses no problem for God. Even back in eternity He would see when the harvest would be ripe for reaping. God "allotted the times" (Acts 17:26, NRSV) of existence and the borders to every nation. In the same way God has specified a certain period of time for humanity on earth before Christ's second advent.

Neither our procrastination of planting the gospel seed nor our sinfulness will obstruct or derail God's plan for our planet or for the universe. God knows the moment for the harvest, and it will be at the time He has seen and set rather than when we think it ought to have been.

By saying that God had to postpone His Son's second coming because of our dalliance, we deprive Him at one stroke of both His foreknowledge and omniscience. In so doing we lower our omniscient God to our own level.

God has not abdicated the throne of the universe, nor has He handed over the management of His work on earth to mortals. He has retained and still retains and will always retain the control of this earth and His mission on it—that "through all the play and counterplay of human interests and power and passions, the agencies of the all-merciful One, silently, patiently working out the counsels of His own will."[3] Let no one think even for one moment that God Himself is not in ultimate control. He is! "There will be a series of events revealing that God is master of the situation,"[4] Inspiration assures us.

---

[1] Ellen G. White manuscript 4, 1883, in *Selected Messages*, book 1, p. 68.

[2] ————, *The Spirit of Prophecy*, vol. 4, p. 291.

[3] ————, *Education*, p. 173.

[4] ————, *Testimonies*, vol. 9, p. 96.

CHAPTER 15

Ellen White on the Delay

The first time Ellen White used the word "delay" in reference to the Second Advent occurred in 1868. "The Lord intimates a delay before the morning finally dawns," she said. Further on, in the same article, she gives the reason for it: "God's unwillingness to have His people perish has been the reason for so long delay."[1]

From that time on the delay-theme cropped up from time to time in her writings. In 1876 she commented, "He [Jesus] delays His coming . . ."[2] During the 1880s it appeared in several versions. In 1882: "For forty years did unbelief, murmuring, and rebellion shut out ancient Israel from the land of Canaan. The same sins have delayed the entrance of modern Israel into the heavenly Canaan."[3] In 1886: "His [Christ's] chariot wheels have been delayed,"[4] and "the coming of the Lord is delayed . . ."[5]

In 1898 she observed that "time delays."[6] Many believers see in such statements evidence that God has chosen to postpone or reschedule Christ's Second Advent.

They find further support for the idea in two of Christ's parables. Both the parable of the faithful and evil Servants (Matt. 24:45-51) and the parable of the wise and foolish virgins (Matt. 25:1-12) seem to indicate a delay.

The parables show that the master and the bridegroom arrived after the time that they had been expected. The King James Version uses the word "delayeth" to describe the lateness of the master's return and "tarried" in the parable about the virgins.

Ellen White's writings are Bible-based. In discussing the atonement, for instance, she did not use the formal models or theories employed by theologians. Instead as background for her discussion of the atonement she referred to the Hebrew sanctuary service, as presented in the Pentateuch (the five books of Moses). As a result her presentation of the atonement is distinct from that of contemporary theologians.

Ellen White's vocabulary is also biblical. Usually she followed the language of the King James Version, using its terms and words. In the parable of the faithful and evil servants, both servants waiting for their master found that he did not come as soon as they had expected him. The evil servant then said [in the King James Version] that his master *delayed* his coming. The ten virgins likewise had to wait longer for the bridegroom than they had assumed. The King James Version says he "tarried," while the New King James Version and both the Revised Standard Version and the New Revised Standard Version declare that the bridegroom "was delayed."

In the Greek the words translated "delayeth" and "tarried" both represent the Greek word *chronizoo*. Several modern versions more aptly translate the meaning of the word in both Matthew 24:48 and 25:5. The New International Version renders the verses as the "master is staying away a long time," and "the bridegroom was a long time in coming."[7]

In other words, in both parables the persons watched for did not arrive as soon as the waiting parties hoped they would come. Neither parable, however, says that the person was actually delayed or had actually postponed his arrival. In these parables the alleged delay existed in the expectations of the people who waited for them.

If one uses the word "delay" in translating the parables, it should be made to refer to those who anticipated the arrival, not to the individuals looked for. It was a personal or subjective delay in the expectations of the people waiting rather than an objective delay in the arrival itself. This is the meaning Ellen White gave the word "delay" the first time she used it in 1868. After saying that "the Lord intimates a delay," she added in the next sentence, "But He would not have them [the Advent believers] give way to weariness, nor relax their earnest watchfulness, because the morning does not open upon them *as soon as they expected*."[8]

The delay our spiritual forebears experienced in waiting for Jesus to return was like that of the two servants and the virgins in the Bible parables. As the master and the bridegroom were a long time away, so Jesus was a long time in coming according to the expectations of the early Advent believers. Ellen White frankly admitted this in 1883 when she wrote, "The angels of God in their messages to men represent time as very short. Thus it has always been presented to me. It is true that time has continued longer than we expected in the early days of the message. Our Saviour did not appear as soon as we hoped."[9]

The Saviour's return was definitely delayed in relationship to the early Advent believers' expectations. But it never posed a problem to Ellen White. She called their waiting for Christ's second advent "the *apparent* tarrying time," and added that it "is not so in reality, for at the appointed time our Lord will come."[10]

Among the meanings of "apparent," *Merriam-Webster's Collegiate Dictionary* lists "appearing as actual to the eye or mind" and "manifest to the senses as real or true on the basis of evidence that may or may not be factually valid."

To early Seventh-day Adventists it seemed that Christ had delayed His second advent, as it does to some today. It is in this sense that Ellen White spoke of delay.

Already in 1879—four years before she made the statement that the work might have been finished and the saints in the kingdom by 1883[11]—Ellen White wrote of *the apparent extension of time* in the following words: "We are now upon the very borders of the eternal world, but it is the purpose of the adversary of souls to lead us to put far off the close of time. . . . Because the time is *apparently extended* . . ."[12] To the eagerly waiting early Adventists it looked as if Christ's coming had been postponed, just as the master's return appeared to have been delayed in the eyes of the evil servant, and the bridegroom's coming to the ten virgins.

A prophecy early Seventh-day Adventists had regarded as applying to the time of the Second Advent was Habakkuk 2:1-4. It advises the prophet to stand on his watch and wait for the fulfillment of the vision "though it tarries."

The Septuagint, the pre-Christian Greek translation of the Old Testament, uses here the word *chronizoo*. Arndt and Gingrich translate this part of Habakkuk 2:3 as "it will fail to come for a long time,"[13] rather than "tarry." As noted previously, it is the same Greek word used for delay and tarrying in the parables about the faithful and evil servants and about the ten virgins. Commenting on Habakkuk 2:3, Ellen White mentioned that before the disappointment of October 22, 1844, no one had "noticed that *an apparent delay* in the accomplishment of the vision—a tarrying time—is presented in the same prophecy."[14]

The word "tarry" in Hebrews 10:37 is also translated from the Greek *chronizoo*. Instead of rendering it "'For yet a little while, and He who is coming will come and will not tarry,'" Arndt and Gingrich interpret the last phrase as "will fail to come for a long time."[15] Ellen White said of the text, "It is plainly implied that there would be a *seeming delay* and that the Lord would appear to tarry."[16]

---

[1] Ellen G. White, *Testimonies*, vol. 2, pp. 192, 194. Ralph E. Neall in *How Long, O Lord?* (Hagerstown, Md.: Review and Herald Pub. Assn., 1988) offers possible reasons for Ellen White's occasional statements on a delay.

[2] Ellen G. White manuscript 5, 1876, in Neall, p. 134.

[3] Ellen G. White, *Selected Messages*, book 1, p. 69.

[4] Ellen G. White letter 21, 1886, in Neall, p. 134.

[5] Ellen G. White letter 84, 1886, in Neall, p. 136.

[6] Ellen G. White manuscript 151, 1898, in Neall, p. 143.

[7] Matthew 24:48: Moffatt—"long of coming"; TEV—"not come back for a long time"; Jerusalem—"taking his time." Luther, in his time, also correctly translated this verse in keeping with these modern translations.

Matthew 25:5: Moffatt—"long of coming"; TEV—"late in coming"; Amplified—"lingered."

[8] Ellen G. White, *Testimonies*, vol. 2, p. 192. (Italics supplied.)

[9] ———, *Selected Messages*, book 1, p. 67.

¹⁰ Ellen G. White letter 38, 1888, in Neall, p. 138. (Italics supplied.)
¹¹ ———, *Selected Messages*, book 1, p. 68.
¹² ———, *Testimonies*, vol. 4, p. 306. (Italics supplied.)
¹³ W. F. Arndt and F. W. Gingrich, *A Greek-English Lexicon of the New Testament* (Chicago: University of Chicago Press, 1957), p. 896.
¹⁴ Ellen G. White, *The Great Controversy*, p. 392. (Italics supplied.)
¹⁵ Arndt and Gingrich.
¹⁶ Ellen G. White, *The Great Controversy*, p. 408. (Italics supplied.)

CHAPTER 16

At the Appointed Time

To Ellen White the delay was but an apparent or seeming one, so she personally found no problem with it. Hence she demurred at and repeatedly remonstrated against anyone suggesting either in word or behavior that anything had postponed Christ's coming. In *Testimony* 23, published in 1873, she said, "Faith in the soon coming of Jesus is waning. 'My Lord delayeth his coming' is not only said in the heart, but expressed in words and most decidedly in works."[1]

Similar statements appeared in 1881: "The warning that the Son of man is soon to come in the clouds of heaven has become to many a familiar tale. They have left the waiting, watching position. The selfish, worldly spirit manifested in the life reveals the sentiment of the heart, 'My Lord delayeth his coming.'"[2]

"Let us beware that we be not swept away by the current of worldliness, thus saying to unbelievers, 'The time is not. Be not alarmed. My Lord delayeth His coming'"[3]

In 1886 she wrote in *The Youth Instructor*: "We have, through searching the Scriptures, come to believe that the end of all things is at hand. This knowledge of the nearness of Christ's coming should not be allowed to lose its force. . . . The rapidly diminishing space of time between us and eternity should more deeply impress us. . . . Are you, my dear readers . . . , saying in your heart, 'My Lord delayeth his coming'?" She noted that "these truths [regarding the nearness of the Lord's coming] have been repeated ofttimes, but they are not an old story until the event transpires."[4]

While in Australia in 1895 Ellen White wrote, "There are many who have outgrown their advent faith. They are living for the world, and while saying in their hearts, as they desire it shall be, 'My Lord delayeth his coming.'"[5]

In 1903: "Let no one say in his heart or by his works, 'My Lord delayeth his coming.' . . . The Lord is soon to come. . . . I feel as if I must cry aloud, 'Homeward bound.' We are nearing the time when Christ will come with power and great glory, to take His ransomed ones to their eternal home."[6]

According to the parable it was the evil servant who said his master had delayed his return (Matthew 24:45-51), not the master or even the narrator. The servant lulled himself into a sense of security so that he could follow his natural human inclinations and enjoy his carefree life in sin. The good and faithful servant made no such suggestion. Later the scoffers during the time of the early Christian church followed the example of the evil servant in mocking the idea of Christ's imminent return (see 2 Peter 3:3, 4).

In a *Review and Herald* article of 1894[7] Ellen White first asked the question why Christ's second coming had been so long delayed. But a few sentences later she spoke disapprovingly of the many voices "saying, 'My Lord delayeth his coming.'" How could Ellen White herself repeatedly speak of a delay and then take others to task for suggesting that Christ had postponed His advent? She felt free to do so since to her it was but an apparent or seeming delay.

The same article also spoke of "the appointed time of the judgment." This of course is in harmony with the apostle Paul's statement that "he [God] has fixed a day on which he will judge the world in righteousness" (Acts 17:31, RSV).

Judgment and Christ's second advent are closely related. In one sense Christ's second coming is part of the judgment, and "the Father has fixed" the time for both by His own authority (see Acts 1:7, RSV).

To Ellen White it posed no problem to speak of a delay of the Second Advent and yet feel hurt when others did so in order to enjoy their carefree life. She recognized it as only an apparent or seeming delay in relation to her and her fellow believers' expectations.

In 1888 she wrote that she and her fellow believers confidently and patiently were "waiting and watching unto prayer, looking for and loving the appearing" of their Saviour. Although disappointed, their faith had not failed, for "the apparent tarrying is not so in reality, for *at the appointed time* our Lord will come."[8]

Again in 1901 Ellen White expressed her belief in *an appointed time* for Christ's return: "There are those who say not only in their hearts, but in all their works, 'My Lord delayeth his coming.' Because Christ's coming has been long foretold, they conclude that there is some mistake in regard to it. But the Lord says, 'The vision is yet for *an appointed time*, but at the end it shall speak, and not lie: though it tarry, wait for it; because it will surely come.'"[9]

God had an appointed or scheduled time for the Babylonians under Nebuchadnezzar to let the sinful Israelites reap what they had sown. Just so He has a time set for Christ's second advent when "He will reward each according to his works" (Matt. 16:27).

God's expectant children have usually tended to think of His promises as being delayed in some way. Abraham never saw God's promise that he would receive Canaan as an inheritance come to fruition in his lifetime. He never owned any part of it—"not even enough to set his foot on" (Acts 7:5). At the death of his wife Sarah he had to buy from the Canaanites a rock-hewn tomb in the cave of Machpelah for his burial place (see Gen. 23:3-20). Ellen White observed, "The fulfillment of God's promise [to Abraham of Canaan as an everlasting possession] may seem to be long delayed . . . ; it may appear to tarry; but *at the appointed time* 'it will surely come, it will not tarry.' Habakkuk 2:3."[10] The appointed time here refers to Christ's coming and the end of the world. And that moment "the Father has fixed by his own authority" (Acts 1:7, RSV).

Children are archetypical believers in immediate action on any announced plan. Most parents have heard a small son or daughter protest, "Daddy/Mommy, you said we were going to do so and so. Why aren't we doing it?"

When you told your son that you were going to put up a basketball hoop on a sheet of plywood on the front of your hip-roofed garage, you never planned to do it that very day. But your little boy expected immediate execution of your announced plan.

To your child's thinking you were delaying doing what you said you'd do. But when you told him/her of your plan, you had in mind some later day—not that very moment. When you did tackle and finish the project, you never conceived of it as postponed. But it definitely seemed delayed to your little son or daughter. With reference to your child there had been a subjective delay, but never an actual objective delay in your fulfillment of your plan.

Relative to the hopes and expectations of God's loyal followers throughout Christian history, there has been a definite subjective delay in Christ's second advent. God's faithful people have been like little children. They have expected Jesus to come in their day. And their attitude pleases God. He wants His spiritual children to be looking for Him always, just as human children watch for their daddy or mommy to come home.

---

[1] Ellen G. White, *Testimonies*, vol. 3, p. 255.

[2] *Ibid.*, vol. 5, p. 9.

[3] ———, in *Review and Herald*, Nov. 29, 1881.

[4] ———, in *The Youth's Instructor*, Aug. 25, 1886.

[5] ———, *Testimonies to Ministers*, p. 77.

[6] ———, in *Review and Herald*, July 14, 1903.

[7] *Ibid.*, Mar. 27. 1894.

[8] Ellen G. White letter 38, 1888, in Neall, p. 138. (Italics supplied.)

[9] Ellen G. White, in *Review and Herald*, June 18, 1901. (Italics supplied.)

[10] ———, *Patriarchs and Prophets*, p. 170. (Italics supplied.)

CHAPTER 17

Human Audacity

Some time ago my wife and I drove to Dulles Airport, near Washington, D.C., to meet our daughter Mari, who was flying in from California. Unfortunately, we failed to call to ascertain if the flight was on time. Arriving a minute or two late because of traffic congestion on I-66, we went directly to the baggage claim area for her flight.

At the baggage area we found only a few people. Assuming the passengers had not yet deplaned, we just waited. But when after a while no passengers showed up, we went to an airline official to learn when the flight would arrive.

He informed us that our daughter's plane was still at O'Hare Airport in Chicago because of engine problems. But it would soon be ready to leave. In time it did land at Dulles after a delay of more than three hours.

Some faithful Adventists are weighed down with deep grief because they believe Christ's second advent has also been delayed. Self-condemnation compounds their sorrow. If Jesus would come the second time even one year earlier, they reason, it would prevent much suffering and misery.

These faithful Advent believers are convinced that they and their church have compelled Jesus to postpone His return, and thus caused additional and unnecessary suffering. Some complain that Jesus procrastinates His coming. But they defend the divine delay by pleading that circumstances beyond God's control have delayed His intervention in human affairs and prevented Jesus' desired return.

To me such claims smack of audacity, even bordering on blasphemy. It implies that we have taken God—the Ruler of the universe—captive. Stymieing God in the execution of His Second Advent, we have thrown His time schedule for the plan of salvation out of sync. Such reasoning is the very acme of arrogance—that sinful humans are able to tie the hands of the Omnipotent One so that He is unable to carry out His plans.

But to hold such a position is to arrogate to oneself too exalted a position. Our personal failure to experience Christ's transforming power and sound the life-transforming gospel invitation can never derail God's plan for Jesus to come at the appointed time—"fixed by His [God's] own authority" (Acts 1:7, RSV).

My wife and I knew that our daughter's flight was delayed. When it finally arrived, we also knew how late it was, because we knew its scheduled arrival time. On the other hand, if the flight had had no set time, we could not have said that it had been postponed.

For anyone to say that an event has been delayed, the person must first know what time the event was originally scheduled for. But no human being has ever been told the time for Christ's second advent. Not even Jesus while on earth knew that moment.

As mortals we should refrain from attributing to the Creator and Ruler of the universe some of our own human limitations. When we say that God and Jesus are dilatory, but blameless because it is not Their fault, we denigrate the Almighty and bring Him down to our own level. We may make such conjectures about mortals, but must be careful not to use that language about the Ruler of the universe.

How much confidence do we have in God? How complete is our trust in Him? Do we rely on Him only on sunny days? Do we accept His power implicitly, or do we resort to and rely on our own intellect? Eve thought she was wise enough to decide between right and wrong. Relying on her own reasoning power, she did not think that anything disastrous had befallen her even after she ate the forbidden fruit.

Faithfulness embraces staying power. It embodies the "patience of hope in our Lord Jesus Christ" (1 Thess. 1:3). Such faithfulness maintains complete trust in God and His plan and personal commitment to Him even though Christ's second advent, like the bridegroom in the parable, is "a long time in coming" (Matt. 25:5, NIV).

The faithful and wise servant in the parable exercised wisdom by trusting the superior understanding and knowledge of his master. Cheerful and ready to serve at all times, he was not pessimistic even if his master had not come as soon as he had hoped. He never let the apparent delay beguile him.

Although the faithful servant knew no more than the evil servant of when his master would return, each day he conscientiously performed his entrusted duties. Each moment he was alert—and ready—for the coming of his lord. No matter when, he was prepared to welcome his master's return with joy. Since he was keenly aware that his days and times were in the hands of his loving master, he was not overly concerned with the particular date of the master's arrival.

After migrating to England, the great German composer, George Frederick Handel, wrote his famous oratorio *Messiah* between August 22 and September 14, 1741. On its first performance in London in 1743 King George II was present. Greatly impressed, the monarch rose to his feet in an act of homage to the unseen King of the universe as the choir swelled into the awe-inspiring "Hallelujah Chorus" that declared "the Lord God Omnipotent reigneth," " 'He shall reign for ever and ever,' " "Hallelujah!"

The psalmist had also internalized that concept, and so he told God's people, "Be still, and know that I am God" (Ps. 46:10). And the prophet Habakkuk, after long agonizing about God's slowness in punishing wicked Judah, arrived at the reassuring awareness that "the Lord is in His holy temple." With the confidence that God is still on the throne of the universe securely abiding in his previously troubled heart, he advised, "Let all the earth keep silence before Him" (Hab. 2:20).

It seems rather brash for mere mortals to say that God has postponed the Second Advent. Particularly so when Ellen White tells us that "the exact time of the second coming of the Son of man is God's mystery."[1] A mystery is a secret or something beyond human knowing or finding out.

God told us through Moses that "the secret things belong to the Lord our God" (Deut. 29:29). Ellen White continued the Mosaic theme by saying that "those things that are revealed we shall accept for ourselves and our children; but let us not seek to know that which has been kept secret in the councils of the Almighty."[2]

Sometimes parents have secrets that they choose not to divulge to their children. If the children get some hint of it and then try to pry it out, the parents do not appreciate their inquisitiveness. It is at least impolite, and well-bred children will refrain from such behavior.

To me it seems likely that God does not appreciate our trying to pry into secrets lodged solely in His own mind. So if we do insist on speaking about a postponement of the Second Advent, we should at least modify it by calling it an "apparent" or "seeming" delay, as Ellen White did (as we noted in the preceding chapter).

It appears utterly incongruous to me that the Creator of the universe should depend on humans to open earth's door so that the Saviour can come back to take His own to the mansions He has prepared for them. If Satan can prevent Him from returning, he certainly would do so forever. But I am glad that the prince of this world does not possess such power.

Instead, Ellen White assures that "there will be a series of events revealing that *God is master of the situation*. The truth will be proclaimed in clear, unmistakable language. . . . Through most wonderful working of divine providence, mountains of difficulty will be removed and cast into the sea. The message that means so much to the dwellers upon the earth will be heard and understood. Men will know what is truth. Onward and still onward the work will advance until the whole earth shall have been warned, and then shall the end come."[3] The opening up of the former U.S.S.R. to the gospel certainly was a removal of such a mountain of difficulty.

Christ's first advent occurred at the time God had planned. But in the thinking of some of His chosen people, Jesus was even dilatory in His arrival as the promised Messiah.

God's clock is always on time. It is never fast nor slow, as ours might be. Nor is God ever tardy, as we sometimes are. He does things on time. "'When the fulness of the time was come, God sent forth his Son.' . . . Providence had directed the movements of nations, and the tide of human impulse and influence, until the world was ripe for the coming of the Deliverer."[4]

So God through providence will also prepare the time for Christ's second advent. The Lord still knows the time. And Christ's return will take place at the moment foreseen in the councils of heaven. Don't for a moment think that you and I can change what has been fixed in God's mind and plan.

Assuming that we have delayed Christ's second advent leads to a fatal consequence. It causes us to focus our eyes on self rather than on God—and Satan could not be more pleased. He knows that Christians who turn their gaze away from God to self will either become like the self-righteous Pharisees (see Luke 18:10-12) or dispirited when they notice how far they fall short of modeling Jesus. Those immersed in despair are an easy prey for Satan and will usually soon leave Christ. As for the Pharisees, they never really belonged to Him, even though they were members of His church.

God wants us to focus our attention not on self, but on Jesus. Only by beholding Him will we be "transformed into the same image from glory to glory, just as by the Spirit of the Lord" (2 Cor. 3:18). Only in this way will we become God's effective helpers in finishing His work on earth.

Human expectations often fail, but not the plans and purposes of God. "Like the stars in the vast circuit of their appointed path, God's purposes know no haste and no delay."[5]

"The world is not without a ruler. The program of coming events is in the hands of the Lord. The Majesty of heaven has the destiny of nations, as well as the concerns of His church, in His own charge.

"We permit ourselves to feel altogether too much care, trouble, and perplexity in the Lord's work. Finite men are not left to carry the burden of responsibility. We need to trust in God, believe in Him, and go forward."[6]

May we all join William Cowper as he courageously sings:

"God moves in a mysterious way
  His wonders to perform;
  He plants His footsteps in the sea,
  And rides upon the storm.
  Ye fearful saints, fresh courage take . . ."

"Alleluia! For the Lord God Omnipotent reigns!" (Rev. 19:6).

---

[1] Ellen G. White, *The Desire of Ages*, p. 633.
[2] ———, *Selected Messages*, book 1, p. 191.
[3] ———, *Testimonies*, vol. 9, p. 96. (Italics supplied.)
[4] ———, *The Desire of Ages*, pp. 31, 32.
[5] *Ibid.*, p. 32.
[6] ———, *Testimonies*, vol. 5, pp. 753, 754.

CHAPTER 18

Fellowship With God

Visiting with a neighbor over the backyard fence several years ago, I asked her, "When your husband was courting you, was there any color he told you he did not like?"

"Green," she answered quickly, almost as by reflex. Then she told me that during their first date their conversation had drifted to the subject of colors, and he had casually mentioned that he did not care for green in clothing.

She confided to me that at the time she had several green outfits, but after learning about her escort's aversion to green, her green clothes got pushed farther and farther back into her wardrobe until she never used them again.

That conversation has lingered in my memory. And I have come to the conclusion that just as there was a definite connection between my neighbor's voluntary adjustment to the wishes of her new acquaintance and their growing friendship, maturing love, and subsequent marriage, so there is also a comparable relationship between God's wishes and our joyful compliance with them. I am persuaded that if you and I are going to spend eternity with God and the angels, we will not only choose to keep His commandments and obey His requirements, but we will also gladly respond to God's further wishes.

This young woman's date could not have forced her to discard her green outfits. She had a perfect right to wear them. If she had wanted to, she could have appeared dressed in green from head to toe for their next date. But she chose not to exercise those rights. She was more interested in cultivating an intimate friendship with her newfound acquaintance. Wanting to please her new friend, she adjusted to his wishes. In this way he became her best friend and future bridegroom and husband.

Obedience by itself is not sufficient to prepare us for joyful fellowship with God and the angels. Such obedience or compliance with requirements may be forced. Slaves are obedient. They may render reluctant or even rebellious obedience while detesting their master's rules and regulations. Those rules may go against the very grain of their inmost beings. But they obey. Such slavelike obedience will not fit us for true fellowship with God and His angels.

A Roman soldier could legally force a Jew to carry a burden for a mile. While doing that, the Jew was a slave. So Jesus advised, "'If one of the occupation troops forces you to carry his pack one mile, carry it two miles'" (Matt. 5:41, TEV). On the second mile the Jew was no longer a slave. The Roman soldier's pack was now carried by choice. So God wants His followers not to be slaves but to be free, for "Christ has set us free" (Gal. 5:1, RSV).

Christians who obey just because the law says they have to do certain things are slaves. On the other hand, those who have responded by faith or trust to the grace of our Lord Jesus Christ and have placed their love and affections on Him and obey God with love and joy are indeed free. Instead of being pushed or coerced into conformity to divine will, they find themselves drawn by divine love.

"The love of Christ constrains us," the apostle Paul tells us in 2 Corinthians 5:14. The New Revised Standard Version renders the phrase as "the love of Christ urges us on." That translation gives a happier rendering. It is the love of Christ that draws us to

Him and imparts to us a glad-hearted desire to follow His will. Genuine Christians are not forced to do God's will by the coercive power of their intellectual understanding of divine truth. Rather, the Holy Spirit has brought the truth to their hearts so that they now will to follow Jesus and go His way.

"All true obedience comes from the heart. It was heart work with Christ. And if we consent, He will so identify Himself with our thoughts and aims, so blend our hearts and minds into conformity to His will, that when obeying Him we shall be but carrying out our own impulses. The will, refined and sanctified, will find its highest delight in doing His service. When we know God as it is our privilege to know Him, our life will be a life of continual obedience. Through an appreciation of the character of Christ, through communion with God, sin will become hateful to us."[1]

Augustine expressed that same sentiment 1,500 years ago when he said, "Love God and do what you like." He meant that as the grace of God transforms a Christian, the person's will becomes aligned with God's will so that he or she enjoys going God's way. Now God's will and the Christian's desires coalesce. They become one and the same. When that becomes your experience and mine, then Jesus' prayer for His disciples "that they also may be one in Us" (John 17:21) has been fulfilled in you and me.

Another time Ellen White phrased this experience in these words: "When we submit ourselves to Christ, the heart is united with His heart, the will is merged in His will, the mind becomes one with His mind, the thoughts are brought into captivity to Him; we live His life."[2]

A little girl had just given her life to Jesus. She rightly understood the nature of conversion and said to her mother, "From now on I am always going to do whatever I want to do."

"Not so, my dear," her mother responded instantly. "From now on you are to do just what God wants you to do."

"Yes," replied her daughter cheerfully. "From now on Jesus and I will want the same things."

She was right. In her conversion experience she had chosen to let the mind of Jesus rule her mind and choices (see Phil. 2:5).

Today we hear a great deal about free choice, but God granted

Adam and Eve—and everyone still today—the right to exercise their free will. All of us may think and do exactly what we please. Every person may choose his or her own way. But if we persist in going our own way by indulging thoughts and cherishing feelings and plans contrary to God's will, as did Lucifer, we will forfeit communion with God now as well as fellowship with Him and the angels for eternity.

The other day I heard a minister say with fervor from the pulpit, "We don't need religion; we need a relationship with Christ." He meant that it is not enough to belong to and attend a church. Rather to experience salvation, a person must know and love Jesus.

The preacher's stirring plea was good. But the word "relationship," so often used today to define a Christian's connection with God, is not adequate to express a person's functional Christian experience.

A philanderer enjoys a one-night stand with a prostitute. But not even such an intimate relationship mirrors a functional Christian relationship with Christ. A philanderer's relationship to the object of his passion lacks both love and commitment—integral components of a genuine Christian relationship with God.

Consequently, a person's relationship as such with God guarantees neither peace of mind nor salvation, either here or for eternity. Satan himself has a definite relationship with both God and Jesus. In the same manner, every person has a relationship with anyone he or she comes in contact with. But such a relationship does not make for soul harmony.

Only love with oneness of mind, purposes, and plans—a present soul communion or fellowship with God—will fit Christians to live with God for eternity and grant them peace of mind as they travel toward His eternal home.

Adam and Eve, God's first children on earth, enjoyed not a mere relationship with God. They fellowshipped with God Himself in their garden home. As they did so, it filled their days with happiness. They took care of the garden and talked with visiting angels. Each day they spent time in joyful meditation on God's love and gifts. "In the cool of the day" (Gen. 3:8, NIV) God Himself would come down and stroll around in the lovely garden with them. Eden was God's garden, but He had entrusted it to them as their home.

Our first parents found life in their garden home enjoyable and invigorating. But they derived their greatest pleasure from their contact with their heavenly visitors—especially God, their heavenly Father. They were comfortable in His company. Love bound them to all their celestial visitors, but most of all to God Himself.

One common tenor of love ran through their thoughts, feelings, plans, and aims, and they loved to please Him by following His suggestions. Because their love and affections centered on Him, they enjoyed doing things His way. This is the kind of fellowship with God the Father and Jesus that awaits us after Jesus takes us to His Father's home.

The apostle John wrote that "if we walk in the light as He [God] is in the light, we have fellowship with one another, and the blood of Jesus Christ His Son cleanses us from all sin," "and truly our fellowship is with the Father and with His Son Jesus Christ" (1 John 1:7, 3).

Such fellowship is more than a relationship. It is soul communion with God. The apostle Paul hinted at this present soul union or fellowship with Jesus when He wrote that His Father has "raised us up with him and seated us with him in the heavenly places in Christ Jesus" (Eph. 2:6, NRSV). The purpose of Christ's death on the cross was to bring about union with Him "so that whether we wake or sleep we might live with Him" (1 Thess. 5:10, RSV).

---

[1] Ellen G. White, *The Desire of Ages*, p. 668.
[2] ———, *Christ's Object Lessons*, p. 312.

CHAPTER 19

Attitude— Not Time— Is Important

The prophet Isaiah says that God has created us for His glory (see Isa. 43:7). The Westminster Catechism does not stop with that. It declares that man's chief end is "to glorify God, and to enjoy him forever."[1] At Creation it was the Lord's plan and hope that every free-willed intelligent being should thoroughly delight in and enjoy God's company and intimate fellowship.

Only as we daily think of and visit with God in the present life will we be fitted for eternal fellowship with God and the angels. Adam and Eve did just that in their sin-free garden home. But one day they disobeyed God. After that, they felt afraid and alienated from Him when He came to visit. God had to close the gates to their lovely garden home. In their sinful state they could no longer appear in the presence of God, for to sin, wherever found, "God is a consuming fire" (Heb. 12:29). To preserve their very lives He must separate them from Him.

Every human being since then has been born alienated from God. We were all born into the wrong family, "by nature children of wrath," "dead in trespasses and sins" (Eph. 2:3, 1). Those who will meet Christ with joy at His second advent will have left the sinful family of the first Adam. Instead they will have followed Jesus' command to Nicodemus: "You must be born again" (John 3:7). "Most assuredly, I say to you, unless one is born of water and the Spirit, he cannot enter the kingdom of God" (verse 5). Born of and indwelt by the Holy Spirit, we will become transformed into "children of obedience" (1 Peter 1:14, ASV).[2] Such "willing and obedient" (Isa. 1:19) followers will enjoy the companionship of God and the angels for eternity and "eat the good of the land."

Before every birthday husband and wife try to discover what his or her spouse wants for a birthday gift. As the mate discovers the wish, he/she endeavors to secure it if it is at all within the realm of reason and possibility. But a spouse certainly never commands his/her mate to buy that certain gift. Neither did the young man compel his friend with the green dresses in her wardrobe to discard them. Rather she chose to do what her friend desired. It was her attitude toward the unenforceable—what he could not have forced her to do—that helped make them best friends and marriage partners for life. Such will be our attitude toward God and His wishes.

Commands or requirements do not really reveal our attitudes, motives, sentiments, or aspirations. Only our attitude and relationship toward the unenforceable accurately discloses them. Many people obey all laws but are not in sympathy with them. For example, they pay their taxes, but grumble about them and the government that collects them. Some Christians pay tithe and give to the church, but do so grudgingly.

God cannot afford to accept such people into His kingdom, although outwardly they obey all His commandments. If they did enter heaven, they would complain even there, just as the driver may obey the speed law but fuss about it all the time. Thus the rebellion against God's government, the annihilation of which demanded the life of His only Son, would start all over again. But that will not happen. "Affliction will not rise up a second time" (Nahum 1:9).

The scribes and Pharisees in the days of Jesus did keep the letter of the law, but they did not do so from the heart. Of them Jesus said: "Unless your righteousness exceeds the righteousness of the scribes and Pharisees, you will by no means enter the kingdom of heaven" (Matt. 5:20).

Have you ever stopped to realize that the major decisions in life occur outside the area of requirements or coercion? They fall in the arena of free choice, the realm of the unenforceable. For example, who compelled you to choose the line of work for which you are currently preparing or are now pursuing? Who coerced you to marry the person now your spouse? And who forced any of us to join the church to which we now belong? No one! No compulsion forced you and me to make any of these decisions. They all resulted from free choice in the area of the unenforceable.

Like you, I want my friendship with Jesus to deepen. Hence, I try to ascertain His will for me, because I desire to please Him. By God's grace my goal is to come to the place where my heart daily beats in unison with His great heart of infinite love.

I grew up in a home where we had meat or fish at least once a day, and often twice. And I did not discard either as soon as I became a Seventh-day Adventist. But with the insight gained I gradually concluded that God wanted me to leave both off my diet, since it would be better for my health.

Just as you and I want to live in good houses—not wretched, dilapidated ones—so I am sure that the Holy Spirit also prefers a good dwelling place. And the "body is the temple of the Holy Spirit who is in you" (1 Cor. 6:19). As a result, I am eager to keep my body in the best possible health so as to make it a comfortable abode for the Holy Spirit.

Although the Seventh-day Adventist Church does not mandate a vegetarian diet, it is its ideal. It is also the diet God gave humans when He created them. And we believe He offered them the best possible one. I therefore choose to follow God's prescription. But in the Seventh-day Adventist Church vegetarianism is not a command; it falls in the realm of the unenforceable—the area of each member's free choice.

As true friends of Jesus, we shall not ask how little we may do and still remain children in our heavenly Father's family. Rather, it will be our constant aim to see how far we can go in fulfilling the wishes of our Friend Jesus and our heavenly Father. It will be the

Christian's aim to emulate our Elder Brother Jesus, who, while He was on earth, said of His Father, "I always do what pleases Him" (John 8:29, NIV). So we too will "do those things that are pleasing in His sight" (1 John 3:22).

Being wholly committed to God and His ways, we will want to fulfill His will with joy and gladness of heart to the extent of our comprehension and knowledge. That means that we will not obey God because we have to, for fear of punishment or desire for reward, but because we love to follow in the footsteps of the Master, who inspired the prophet to declare, "I delight to do Your will, O my God, and Your law is within my heart" (Ps. 40:8). Such will also be our constant aim as we live in the New Covenant experience (see Eze. 36:26, 27).

In this way our attitude toward Jesus and His second advent will be one of waiting and longing. But we should avoid the attitude manifested by a man who came to Ellen White and said, "Sister White, do you think the Lord will come in 10 years?"

"What difference does it make to you whether He shall come in two, four, or 10 years?"

"Why, I think I would do differently in some things than I now do if I knew the Lord was to come in 10 years."

"What would you do?" Ellen White asked.

"Why, I would sell my property and begin to search the Word of God and try to warn the people and get them to prepare for His coming, and I would plead with God that I might be ready to meet Him."

"Then if you knew that the Lord was not coming for 20 years, you would live differently?"

He answered, "I think I would."

"Then you know your Master's will, and it is your duty to do just as though you knew that He was coming in [10] years."[3]

In 1887 Ellen White wrote, "The shortness of time is frequently urged as an incentive for seeking righteousness and making Christ our friend. This should not be the great motive with us; for it savors of selfishness. Is it necessary that the terrors of the day of God should be held before us, that we may be compelled to right action through fear? It ought not to be so. Jesus is attractive. He is full of love, mercy, and compassion. He proposes to be our friend, to walk with us through all the rough pathways of life. He says to us, I am the Lord thy God; walk with Me, and I will fill thy path with light. Jesus, the Majesty of heaven, proposes to elevate to companionship with Himself those who come to Him with their burdens, their weaknesses, and their cares."[4]

Jesus loves us. He loves you and me as individuals. May you and I personally respond to the pleadings of the Holy Spirit and cherish a longing in our hearts to become His special friends, as the young woman with the green dresses desired to become her escort's special friend.

---

[1] See Philip Schaff, *The Creeds of Christendom*, sixth ed., rev. and enlarged (Grand Rapids: Baker Book House, first published in 1877 by Harper), vol. 2, p. 787, cf. p. 785.

[2] This is the literal translation of the original Greek, rather than the common rendering, which reads "obedient children." There may well be a difference between "obedient children" and "children of obedience." A child may, like a slave, be obedient because of fear of punishment for disobedience or of reward for obedience. The phrase "children of obedience," on the other hand, conveys the meaning that they are obedient as a result of their nature rather than from any ulterior motives.

[3] See Ellen G. White manuscript 10, 1886.

[4] Ellen G. White, in *Signs of the Times*, Mar. 17, 1887.

Almost Home

I gave my life to God in pre-World War II Europe. At that time I thought Jesus would come within a couple years. Hitler was flexing his military muscles, and the world seemed on the verge of war. After my graduation from Newbold College in England, church leaders advised me to go to the United States to finish college. Since that would take two more years, I protested, saying that by that time Jesus would surely come.

The wise man who urged me to finish college did not refute my belief in the soon return of Jesus. Instead he answered only that he who had been preparing for service would receive the same reward as he who had served. So I came to the United States and graduated from Emmanuel Missionary College, now Andrews University, in the spring of 1940. After that I went to the Seminary and earned my M.A.

By the latter part of the 1940s I was teaching religion at Union College. I had married, and we had two children. As a family we carried no life insurance. So when Social Security opened up for admission of self-employed people (gospel ministers are considered self-employed), my wife, Mae, and I discussed its advisability. When I joined Social Security, I never expected to collect a penny from it. But I entered the program so that in case I died, my wife would get some financial help in rearing our two girls.

Today I have drawn Social Security for many years. Time has lasted much longer than I expected. But I still believe we are treading on the brink of eternity, a conviction reenforced by the unexpected developments that have recently reshaped Communist Eastern Europe and the rapid spread of the three angels' messages with the fulfillment of Matthew 24:14, the difinitive sign of Christ's soon coming in glory.

We are living in days when the political and ideological landscape of nations may change like a kaleidoscope. What we thought durable or permanent can alter in days, as demonstrated by the crumbling of the Berlin Wall and the collapse of the once-mighty U.S.S.R.

As Seventh-day Adventists we have reason to rejoice. The hope of the believers in the Advent throughout the ages is about to be fulfilled. Jesus will soon step out of heaven and return to receive His own. The iron curtain no longer bars the spread of the gospel. The calamities and the problems facing our earth and its inhabitants are numerous. Widespread pollution causes vegetation and even forests to die, AIDS threatens to depopulate whole countries (particularly in Africa),* financial instability or catastrophe looms among nations, and everywhere we see "men's hearts failing them from fear" (Luke 21:26). Each is but an omen that Jesus is soon to come. Jesus said, "Now when these things begin to happen, look up and lift up your heads, because your redemption draws near" (verse 28). The long detour of sin is about to end. Jesus is about to come to claim His children.

Confidently and joyously we can sing with S. J. Graham:

> "The golden morning is fast approaching;
> Jesus soon will come
> To take His faithful and happy children
> To their promised home.
> O, we see the gleams of the golden morning
> Piercing through this night of gloom!
> O, we see the gleams of the golden morning
> That will burst the tomb."

But the particular moment for the Second Advent is not of utmost importance. It is rather our attitude toward God and our gladhearted acceptance of His will, mirrored in our thoughts, actions, and habits, that matters. When we walk with God today—and every day—as did Enoch for 300 years (Gen. 5:22, 24), we will be waiting and longing like a southern California physician I visited with some time ago. As our conversation turned to the happenings of the day, he said, "I really wish Jesus would come!"

My response was "Why do you want that so fervently? To me it appears that your life and conditions are just about ideal. You have a fine family with all enjoying good health, own a comfortable home, and have a good practice yielding you a good income. As far as I can see, you have all you might wish for. You even have a new beautiful church here, where both you and your wife are active and respected."

"I see so much pain and suffering, and so much sin," he instantly replied. Then he told me that on a recent night he had been awakened and called to a motel to care for a young man's fun-loving overnight female companion in desperate on the spot need of medical help. Seeing so often sin with its resultant suffering, he longed for Jesus to come so that the reign of sin and suffering might end. This physician's heart and hope were already in heaven. To him the words of Jesus applied when He said, "For indeed, the kingdom of God is within you" (Luke 17:21). If the longings of our hearts are already in heaven, we will be glad to meet Jesus in person any moment in order to go with Him to His kingdom. We will be like the prospective groom. The sooner the wedding ceremony comes, the better.

With that attitude toward the Second Advent, we will today fellowship with Jesus in our thoughts and live so as to be an honor to Him. We will be like the prospective groom who fellowships with his fiancée in thought and lives so as to be an honor to her. In this way we will aim not only to be blameless, but praiseworthy; not merely to be acceptable, but excellent; not merely to do what is permissible, but what is honorable; not merely to be common, but holy—all as we wait for our Friend and Saviour.

---

* See Richard W. Goodgame, M.D., "Aids in Uganda—Clinical and Social Features," *New England Journal of Medicine* 323, No. 6 (Aug. 9, 1990): 383-389.

Scriptural Index